YOUR FUTURE IN REAL ESTATE

Dedication

To Joseph Durst whose ethics and vision
have been a source of inspiration to those
who look to the real estate industry
as a means of employment
and self-expression.

SEYMOUR B. DURST

To my wife, Donata, whose understanding outlook
on the problems of choosing a career
and pursuing it successfully has been immeasurably
helpful to me in my own career as well as in
evaluating those contained in these pages.

WALTER H. STERN

**ARCO-ROSEN
CAREER GUIDANCE SERIES**

YOUR FUTURE IN
REAL ESTATE

Seymour B. Durst & Walter H. Stern

arco
New York

333.33
D966y

First Arco Printing, 1971

Published by ARCO PUBLISHING COMPANY, INC.
219 Park Avenue South New York, N.Y. 10003
by arrangement with Richards Rosen Press, Inc.

Revised Edition

Library of Congress Catalog Card Number 74-114102
Dewey Decimal Classification 371.42
ISBN 0-668-02264-7

Manufactured in the United States of America

About the Author

SEYMOUR B. DURST.   Seymour B. Durst shares the task of running the Durst Organization, a prominent New York City building firm, with his two brothers and their father. During and after World War I, the elder Durst was a realty investor, but with the great building boom that followed World War II, Seymour and his brothers convinced him that their future lay not in investing but in building. That settled, they looked around for some likely building sites, and, in a decision that made real-estate history, finally chose Third Avenue—then a dilapidated thoroughfare bisected by a noisy, dirty elevated railway. Although this seemed a most unlikely location, the Dursts disposed of many of their choicest properties and, at great risk, spent the money on Third Avenue's run-down tenements. Later, the "El" was torn down, Third Avenue went up and up and up in both appearance and value, and today it ranks as one of the country's leading executive-office centers. Naturally, the Durst Organization also now ranks as one of the largest owners and dealers in Third Avenue property.

Born in New York in 1913, Mr. Durst took a degree in business administration at the University of Southern California. Today a widower, he lives in a suburb of New York City with his four children (who have become accomplished builders on a miniature scale), and commutes to his office, which, of course, is in a Third Avenue skyscraper.

25696

About the Author

WALTER H. STERN. The task of making the complex ins and outs of real estate clear and concise to the layman has for some years been Walter H. Stern's daily concern as a reporter, specializing in real estate, on the staff of The New York *Times*. He joined the *Times* shortly after World War II and, for a few years, covered a wide variety of assignments. Born in Frankfurt am Main, Germany, in 1924, Mr. Stern came to this country in 1936. After getting his B.A. in journalism at New York University, where he was managing editor of the *Washington Square College Bulletin,* the student paper, he was editor of the Forest Hills *Post* and a group of affiliated weekly newspapers published in Queens County. Before joining the *Times,* he worked as a reporter for a news agency that served a number of New York dailies. At college, his second interest was music and, since his senior year, Mr. Stern has served as music critic and radio-and-television editor of the *Musical Leader,* a national magazine published in Chicago. When he and his wife are not spending their leisure time with their two children at their home on Long Island's North Shore, they enjoy playing tennis and listening to classical music at concerts or on hi-fi. Mr. Stern is also capable of sitting down at the piano and batting out just about any major show tune of the last forty years.

Contents

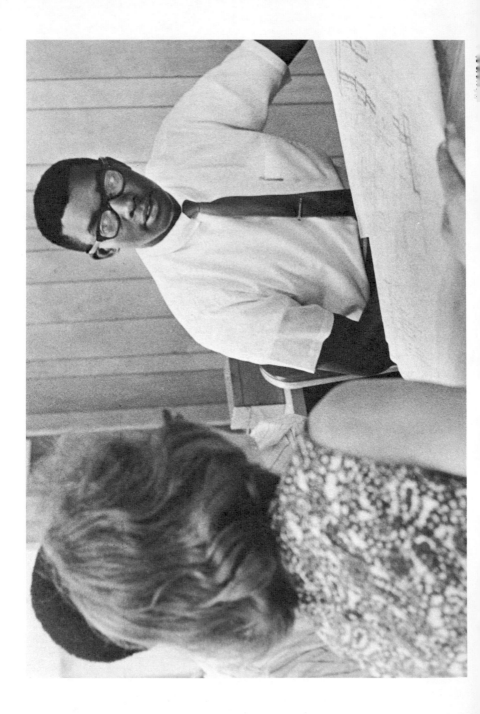

CHAPTER I

The Field

A dapper young man in his late thirties whisked along the Camino Real, just south of San Francisco, in a trim convertible. He turned off at San Mateo and followed a small street a couple of blocks to a neat little white-stucco building with a large plate-glass window in which a neon sign quivered nervously. He parked his car in the adjoining lot and walked briskly into the bustling activity of a busy real-estate agency. Half a dozen salesmen, who were busily doing paper work or talking on the phone, waved a casual greeting to him as he made his way to his private office, an unpretentious but comfortable room in the rear.

This is the young man's last stop on a daily tour of some two dozen real-estate offices he owns on the peninsula below San Francisco. The San Mateo office is his home base, the place where less than ten years ago he began a phenomenal growth that resulted in his becoming the area's leading residential broker. The agility with which Californians buy and sell their homes whenever a move to another neighborhood seems advisable has made him a man of modest wealth. But he does not hesitate to talk about the lean years. He does so now—to a young salesman who hesitatingly knocks on the door frame before entering the private office. The door itself is always open.

"Come on in, Joe," the boss said, with a smile.

9

"I just want to see you for a moment about the Billings house," the salesman explained.

"I thought you had that sold yesterday."

"So did I," the salesman replied. "But this morning Mrs. Billings called and said her husband won't throw in the refrigerator and clothes drier at the price the Joneses offered, so I'm stuck."

"Don't lose any sleep over it, Joe," the boss said. "Call Jones and tell him what happened and see if he won't offer two hundred dollars more if the appliances are included. If he agrees, call Mrs. Billings back and tell her about the new offer. And if she balks, remind her that it isn't easy to sell that house of hers at this price with the small mortgage she's got left on it. That'll bring her around, I'm sure."

"Good idea," the salesman said, and, with a discouraged shake of his head, added, "There must be an easier way to make a living."

"I don't know about that, Joe," the boss replied. "I thought so, too, when I had a job as a car salesman, and then I figured I'd try real estate instead. There are obstacles in any business when you want to make a deal. You'll find that after a while it'll be second nature to you to straighten out little kinks like the appliance question. And sometimes a deal will fall through because you can't get a couple of people to agree on terms. So you start all over again, or work on another house."

"I guess you're right," the salesman said. "How'd you get started in this business, anyhow?"

"That's simple," the boss answered, and leaned back in his swivel chair, obviously ready to launch into his narrative. "When I got fed up with working for someone else, especially selling cars, I decided to go into business for myself," he went on. "Frankly, I didn't care particularly what business it was, but it had to be something where I'd need a minimum of ready cash since I had so precious little. So I decided on real estate. I knew that all I'd have to pay for in advance was a month's rent on a small store, a month's deposit on the phone, a second-hand typewriter, a used desk, two or three chairs, and a filing cabinet. But before I could be a licensed broker I had to put in a couple of years working for another broker as a salesman, as you're doing now. During those years I not only worked to qualify for my license, but I learned those little lessons about Mrs. Billings's icebox. Eventually I opened my first office right here. Of course, in those days this was just a little shack—right where we're sitting—but I added on as things went well and I needed more space. Then, as you know, I went down the peninsula and opened the other branches."

"Think I could do the same one of these days?" the salesman asked.

"You're just the type of guy who could," the boss replied. "You'd make a tough competitor, too, once you learn about Mrs. Billings's icebox. Go ahead, give her a buzz."

Three thousand miles away, another young man leaned back in his leather-covered swivel chair, telephone in hand. By the way he gazed across his smartly carpeted and furnished office, through the tinted, floor-to-ceiling windows overlooking New York's skyscrapers to the west, one might think he was trying to catch a glimpse of the building that was being described to him by the voice on the other end of the line. But while he could not see the building, which dominates the skyline of a Midwestern city, his mind was conjuring up a tempting picture. It was not a picture of the towering structure; he had seen that before. Rather, it was a maze of six-digit figures that, once arranged into proper order by a real-estate investor, suggested a prospect of substantial income that could be derived from ownership.

The man on the phone is one of a growing number of professional real-estate investors and heads of investment companies who today provide the means by which thousands of Americans are sharing in the ownership of impressive properties—office skyscrapers, apartment projects, industrial parks, hotels, motels, and shopping centers. At almost a moment's notice, he will hop a jet to the other end of the country, where, with nothing more than a handshake, he may seal a multi-million dollar bargain, leaving the detailed contracts to be worked out by his lawyers later.

In a medium-sized city in the Midwest, a burly young fellow dressed in a rough pair of slacks, a plaid sport shirt and a lumber jacket left his comfortable home at an early hour and drove off in his mud-caked, late-model car. On the rear seat was a heavy plumber's wrench holding down a wad of rolled-up blueprints. Lying across the floor was a fluorescent lighting fixture he had picked up the night before to replace one that was damaged during construction. On the floorboard next to him was a stack of vari-colored bricks held together by a metal strap. His morning trip was a short one. Soon he turned off the country road and bounced his car across roughly packed earth in a roller-coaster ride that would do a Jeep proud.

This man is a builder. As his healthy tan shows, he spends many of his working hours outdoors, climbing over wood planks, spreading out blueprints on concrete foundations, or making hasty calculations on the back of an envelope with a pile of lumber for a desk. Despite his somewhat unpolished appearance during the working day and the less-than-plush office he maintains in a construction shack or trailer, he is a man who combines imagination and planning—in an immediate physical way—to gain great personal satisfaction as well as a good living from his work.

The foregoing glimpses are just a small, random sampling of the many careers open in the field of real estate. Minds and personalities of all kinds have their place in the realty world. The painstaking blend of quick mathematical calculation and sharp-eyed observation that characterize the art of appraising; the alert judgment needed for mortgage financing; or the resourceful salesmanship that spells success for the broker in selling and leasing commercial real estate— these are a few of the varied branches of real estate.

Two simple observations indicate the vastness of the real-estate world. One is that, except for the hobo who sleeps on a park bench and never works, every man, woman, and child is involved in real estate. That is, the place where we live, work, or seek our leisure involves real property in some form. Another is that when we assess the nation's total wealth—including every item of value, large or small—we find that more than half of it consists of real estate: land, the improvements that have been built on land, and the various other uses to which land has been put. What a challenge for a young man just starting out in business.

Real estate, it might be mentioned, is one of the few fields in which one can readily go from general practice to a specialty or vice versa. And while the staple of its inventory—land—is unchanging, there are few industries in which styles, concepts, and methods can change as thoroughly, though slowly and almost unnoticeably, as in the realty world. The lure a broker held out last year to a prospective office tenant may hold no charms as he tries to make a similar deal today. The mortgage that was easily placed in last month's transaction has now become a challenge on which pivots the success of this month's deal. The qualifications for various careers in the real-estate field may differ from specialty to specialty, but none is so constant and necessary as alertness—both to opportunities and changing trends.

Interestingly enough, though land has been an important commodity from time immemorial, some of the greatest refinements of the real-estate business have been products of the past two generations. Only recently have colleges and universities added this field to their programs. The licensing of real-estate brokers, now required by statute in thirteen states, was unheard of scarcely more than a generation ago. What does this mean to the young man or woman about to choose a profession? It is a clear indication that there is a great reservoir of careers that await ambitious, clearheaded young people with a variety of personalities and educational backgrounds.

Before we put the many possible real-estate careers under the microscope for detailed examination, let us take a look at an average, balanced community to find out how real property fits into the organization of that community.

We have, first of all, a growing number of private homes, rental apartment houses, and residential coöperatives to accommodate a growing population. Then there is the community's business life—the retail merchants on Main Street and in the outlying shopping center as well as the local industry from which many of the residents earn their livelihood. To provide this community with essential services, the local government levies a tax on real estate in proportion to its value. Lastly, there is the factor of community growth, which depends in part on how successfully financial institutions convert idle funds into fiscal energy for production and expansion. In each of these aspects of community life there are career opportunities for the man or woman interested in real estate.

When a private home or apartment house is built, somebody has to first assemble the necessary land. This may involve negotiations conducted by a realty broker, probably one who specializes in land deals. And prior to offering a vacant tract to a prospective builder or developer, the broker or his client may have engaged a surveyor to ascertain the precise limits of the site that is for sale. Here, already, are two professional experts who play an important part in the real-estate life of a community.

Before the builder of, say, a group of private dwellings can go ahead, he must get a financial institution—a bank, a savings-and-loan association, an insurance company—to agree to provide a mortgage for the project when it is completed. Without such an arrangement, he would be hard put to obtain a temporary construction loan while the building is in progress or to sell the houses to individual owner-occupants. Therefore, he goes to see the mortgage officer of a lending institution—another real-estate expert whose specialty is to study the builder's proposals and judge whether the institution's investment in a mortgage is a prudent one in terms of the risk and the worth of the project as an addition to the community. His judgment depends on many things, some of them not directly associated with real estate in the layman's mind. They include a knowledge of economics in general and the money market in particular; insight into the American housewife's often-exercised right to change her mind about where her family ought to reside and what amenities a home should provide; and a long-range view of what can and does happen to neighborhoods over a span of years and how these changes may affect property values.

Once the builder has obtained a mortgage commitment, he begins to translate into brick and mortar the blueprints drawn by his architect, who practices on the outer borders of the real-estate world. The actual construction work in all likelihood will be in the hands of a general contractor, who is another member of the realty family, though a somewhat distant relative. After the houses or apartments are completed, a realty broker will probably come into the picture. With his staff of trained salesmen, he is a specialist in selling and renting houses or apartments.

In the realm of commerce and industry, the realty man also plays a large role. The management of a town's store and office buildings provides a full-time occupation for many enterprising people in the field. Those with a creative urge may conclude that their city's downtown shopping facilities are no longer adequate for the needs of the region—particularly for the increasing number of residents in the outlying sections of town; thus, matters of this sort satisfy their creative mood by planning and constructing those far-flung shopping centers that are springing up all over the nation today. Here, again, the builder works with architects, with mortgage experts, with renting agents, and with real-estate brokers specializing in retail stores.

When it comes to a community's industrial life, there is a dedicated breed of realty man known as the industrial realtor. His activities are manifold. He is the man who first interests a manufacturer in opening his research, production, or warehouse facilities in a given community. Through conferences with his industrial client, he familiarizes himself with his client's requirements. His objective is to find the best-suited premises —a plant that may already be in existence but vacant, or a well-located site on which a new plant can be built. All this involves a practical knowledge of transportation by rail, road, air, or waterway, because most industries are heavily dependent on facilities for bringing in their raw materials and shipping out their finished products. When the industrial realtor has found a suitable site, he negotiates with its owner and, once the deal is set, goes ahead and arranges for the necessary mortgage financing. Sometimes he may have to line up a group of investors—especially if the purchase is a big one—and they will own the plant, which they will lease at a profit to the manufacturer as their tenant. Industrial real-estate deals, it is obvious, can be a challenge to a real-estate man's imagination and ingenuity.

To provide the community with its various essential services, as we said at the outset, local government must levy taxes against real property, and this is always in proportion to the value of each parcel, whether it is residential or commercial. As a result, every town or city needs experts who are able to judge the relative value of local properties. This is the job of the assessor —a specialist in the profession of appraising. But appraising goes far beyond assessing taxes. Some appraisers are also part-time realty brokers while others concentrate on this specialty, but in either case they have their work cut out for them in a thriving community. They are called upon to set the market values of properties for many purposes. One is to assure prospective buyers or sellers of real estate that the price they are offering or asking is realistic. Another is to aid mortgage officers of lending institutions to figure out what size loan a given property merits. A third function of the appraiser arises in condemnations. When a municipality—or a state or the federal government—needs somebody's property for a public improvement, such as a highway, a park, or the like, it can use the right of eminent domain to condemn that property and take title to it. The owner is paid a sum of money that is approved by the courts as equal to the property's value. To determine this value requires the services of an appraiser. Often, however, disputes arise when the owner of a condemned parcel claims that the award is not sufficient. In such event, the owner, too, may retain an appraiser to establish the value. Both appraisers then testify as experts to help the court decide what is fair compensation.

From all this it should be apparent that when a man says "I'm in the real-estate business," he has only given the vaguest clue about the nature of his work. Consequently, there is no single educational program one can follow in preparation for all possible real-estate careers. Nor is every personality suited to every pursuit within the realm of real estate. The outgoing type of man may be more likely to succeed by using his salesmanship as a broker than as an appraiser, where the emphasis is on detailed study and analysis. Conversely, many a successful appraiser would be hard put to engage in the wheeling and dealing that is often required of brokers or investors who deal in large commercial properties. The ability to make and shoulder the responsibility for critical decisions may qualify a man for a career as real-estate investor, operator, or manager; this is no field for the fence-sitter who finds it difficult to sign on the dotted line for fear he may discover later that he has acted imprudently. And while not every builder leads the rugged outdoor life (many of them operate out of comfortable, permanent offices), it is probably not wise for anyone to enter the construction industry if the tumult and the necessity for often being on the job seem repugnant.

There is no hard-and-fast pattern by which men prepare themselves for careers in real estate. The fact that many practitioners in all phases of the industry have followed in their fathers' footsteps is an indication that it helps to be steeped in the business as a tradition. But there are just as many first-generation realty men who have scaled the ladder to success. And while some successful operators in realty have advanced degrees in the field, there is abundant evidence that other men have attained enviable records with little more than the three Rs. If broad educational background is an asset to a realty man nowadays—as it is in nearly every pursuit—this can be put down to the fact that it enables him to deal on an equal footing with clients whose own backgrounds include some advanced studies or whose businesses and real-estate needs are highly complex. In addition to the general benefits to be obtained from a liberal-arts college curriculum, there are now considerably more opportunities for practical specialized education than in the past. Undergraduate programs that include courses in the real-estate business are now being offered in seventy-one major colleges and universities. An additional forty-six institutions have graduate courses leading to advanced degrees in real estate, while many others offer extension courses, which, though they do not lead to degrees, give practical direction to anyone who wants a real-estate career. Moreover, adult-education classes sponsored by civic groups are being given in the evening at innumerable elementary and high schools. For more intensive study of the realty field—primarily for rapid, practical instruction designed to help applicants pass state tests for brokers' licenses—there are twenty-six business schools throughout the country. Most of them offer real-estate subjects along with business courses that include accounting, advertising, and the like. A few offer realty training alone.

But even without a formal specialized education, there are many avenues to a career in real estate. One of the most commonly heard complaints among elderly real-estate executives nowadays concerns the lack of young talent needed to replace the outgoing generation. On this ground, many of the larger realty concerns have taken a cue from large retail, financial, and other business organizations, and have organized training programs. Some of them require that applicants have college educations before they can take in-company training. Other firms, however, require only that the trainee can cope with the day-to-day techniques of business life—well-organized business letters and memorandums, quick calculations in basic arithmetic, and a certain amount of social tact and ease. But regardless of the requirements of individual training programs, the theory behind them is the age-old apprentice system, which holds that there is no place to learn a business faster and more thoroughly than in actual practice. To this end, apprentices, or trainees as the twentieth-century businessman prefers to call them, join their seniors in all phases of real-estate activity; at first, of course, they merely watch an experienced operator at work, but if the trainee makes the grade, his or her initiative will come to the fore and produce what professionals consider a worthwhile new member of the business.

This brings us to the jackpot question. What kind of income can a young man or woman expect to derive from a lifetime spent in the real-estate profession? Needless to say, there is no pat answer. For one thing, there are so many phases of the industry that precise figures must bear more detailed treatment in later pages. For another, we all know that in any field there are successes and failures. Just as we know of realty men who hop from one city to another in their private airliners, stay at giant hotels that they own, and wherever they travel work in office buildings that are part of their operation, we also know of the broker who hopes that Mr. Jones will make up his mind about buying that house this week because on this depends the commission that has already been pledged to the landlord, the grocer, and the gas-station operator. However, it is safe to say that an intelligent young man or woman who is willing to work conscientiously and is capable of some resourcefulness need not be concerned about the latter extreme. Depending on the chosen specialty, the particular community, and the ups and downs of the nation's economy, capable young realty men can plan on being able to provide comfortably for a family of average size. In addition, there is a good chance they will achieve a measure of financial prestige in their community.

More important in a way than potential income is the flexibility of the field. This allows a versatile realty man to aim in the most lucrative direction without subjecting his business organization to violent upsets. For example, a man who finds that buying and selling older income properties is no longer as profitable as building new ones, can become a builder almost overnight, using his staff and physical facilities to good advantage. Similarly, the builder who feels that the time has come to consolidate his holdings and manage them for maximum income can easily convert his operation into a management firm. Nor is it rare for a broker with a general practice to become a specialist. For instance, success with one or two industrial-brokerage deals may bring increasing numbers of industrial listings to an agent who previously dealt in all types of properties. And—here is where the business promises financial rewards—there is often an opportunity for the versatile broker to participate in developing such income-producing projects as shopping centers, industrial parks, or colonies of homes.

Similar opportunities also beckon other members of the real-estate fraternity. Appraisers, for example, can branch out into consulting practices that often command substantial fees. And if mortgage brokers can raise the necessary funds, they can go into the business of warehousing mortgage loans; that is, they make loans with their own funds when the market is poor and then sell these mortgages to lending institutions when it is good. Or they can become primary or secondary lenders, with highly attractive income possibilities.

When we referred above to the real-estate fraternity, we did not use the term idly. Members of the realty profession have a fraternal outlook, regardless of whether they are, in any given case, active in the more fraternal aspects such as local real-estate boards or allied organizations. This is true because, even though business methods differ throughout the country, the basic commodity is the same—land and the improvements built on it. Many realty men (over sixty-five thousand of them, in fact) find it both pleasurable and useful to be members of their local boards and, by virtue of this membership, of the National Association of Real Estate Boards. Within this association, there are many specialized groups, covering such fields as appraisal, property management, industrial development, and others. Then there are national associations for home builders, mortgage bankers, building owners and managers, and various other special-interest groups.

How much attraction these professional associations hold for the average realty man depends largely on local conditions and his general desire to get together with other men in the field. One advantage of being a joiner in this case is that in the realty business the professional association is also a clearing house for information that can be of direct dollars-and-cents benefit to a member. Because the activities of realty people in different specialties are so often interrelated and because some of the most rewarding deals often involve parties at opposite ends of the nation, an information network maintained by a trade association is extremely helpful at times.

From all this it should be clear that we cannot draw the picture of a composite human being and describe it as the portrait of the typical real-estate man. There is no typical real-estate man. But by examining some of the more important branches of the industry, as we shall in the pages following, we can get a clearer picture of the life that lies ahead in the various areas of the realty profession.

CHAPTER II

Residential Brokerage

There is doubtless no other industry in the nation in which the middleman plays as dominant a role as he does in real estate. This is due, in large part, to the bulk of the commodity concerned being not a newly produced item but one that has been in existence for a long time. The commodity, of course, consists of land and the improvements that have been built on it. The improvements—an endless variety of buildings for thousands of uses—are man-made, to be sure, but they are among man's most long-lived creations. As a result, real property tends to survive not only its owners but also its original use.

Thus, we see a home change hands because its owners have outgrown it, passed on, or for any of a number of other reasons. And we see a car barn converted into a television studio because the trolley has passed into history and a new communications medium has been born. Or a tract of barren land, once rented cheaply for a traveling circus's week-long stand, becomes choice acreage for an airport as the age of the big tent gives way to the era of the giant hangar. An industry that depends so heavily on exchange, depends to the same degree on the middleman—the broker who will find the seller a buyer who needs the property. When a man declares that he is in the real-estate business, therefore, the safest guess we can make is that he is a broker.

24

If we compare the real-estate world to the hierarchy in an ant hill, we can liken the broker to the worker ant. He represents the majority of the industry. What is more, most of the other careers in real estate can be pursued more successfully by the man with experience as a broker. Thus, brokerage is both an end and a means to other ends. For this reason, we shall examine the realty brokerage field in the minutest detail. And detail it deserves because of its diversity.

A real-estate broker is an agent who helps the part or sole owner of real property to convert his share into cash or some other item of value by finding a taker who is willing and able to pay what is asked. For this service the broker is paid a commission by whoever hired him to perform it. (In the majority of instances, brokers are retained and paid by the owners, though in special cases the taker foots the bill.) The commission usually represents a percentage of the price the property brings. And we might add here that while the broker is usually the agent of the party disposing of the property, his association with the prospective takers is normally by far the more intimate, because they are the ones that have to be satisfied. It must be obvious by now that we have avoided the use of the terms "seller" and "buyer" or "landlord" and "tenant" and substituted "owner" and "taker" for them. This is because there are many ways to own an interest in real property and just as many ways to transfer such an interest. For example, owning property outright and selling it for cash to somebody else is one of them. Another is to own a piece of property and to lease it to someone for temporary possession. Still another is to get possession of a piece of real estate by leasing it from its owner; then that possession can be sold in the form of a leasehold to a third person, or he can be given temporary rights by means of a sublease. Moreover, there are interests

in real estate that do not give their owner the right
of possession at all—mortgages, for instance. And a
mortgage can be sold by its holder to somebody else for
any suitable amount. A real-estate broker can engage
in arranging the transfer of all types of interests in property, or he can make one of them his specialty.

In theory, anyone is able to act as a real-estate
broker, provided that all principals in the transaction
agree. An unlicensed layman, however, cannot claim
a commission for his work; this is a right reserved for
licensed real-estate brokers under state laws in effect
throughout the United States. These laws differ in detail from one state to another, but their basic intent and
effects are the same. They provide, first of all, that a
broker must display his license so that anyone using
his services is aware from the start that a commission
can and most likely will be charged for these services.
Furthermore, the license assures the broker's client that
the broker has a basic understanding of his function and
of real-estate practices necessary for carrying a deal
through to a successful conclusion. This assurance stems
from the requirement that a candidate for a license
must pass an examination in realty theory and practice
and must have a certain amount of practical experience as a realty salesman or trader before he can take
the examination. And, finally, licensing laws enable
states to enforce standards of ethics; that is, a license
can be withheld or withdrawn if the applicant or owner
is proved unworthy because of violations of the law, un-
ethical dealings, or, in some states, even moral turpi-
tude. And while these laws confront the broker with
many "don'ts," they also endow him with some substantial rights. The most important of these, of course,
is his livelihood—the right to a commission. If a broker
is the agent through whom an interest in real estate has

been transferred from one person to another, and if the broker has complied with the law by making his professional status known to all concerned, he has a legal claim to his commission, a claim that the courts zealously uphold.

Because the various state laws make practical experience in the realty business a requirement for taking the brokerage examination, most states do not have specific educational requirements. After all, it is safe to assume that a person who has successfully negotiated realty deals for, say, two years and who can pass a written examination has mastered the three Rs, and it does not matter much where this knowledge was acquired. Those states that do require a high-school diploma undoubtedly do so to avoid embarrassing an aspiring real-estate broker by making him submit to a literacy test. At present, no states require a college degree for a license.

However, it is obvious that a broad scholastic background is an asset in any career, including real-estate brokerage. On the other hand, a general high-school education is often sufficient for success in many phases of realty brokerage. There certainly is no rule of thumb when it comes to outlining an educational program for a career as a broker. But we venture to say that a college program in either the liberal arts or business will be a substantial benefit for the future real-estate broker. If it is a liberal-arts curriculum, then it is immaterial which of the arts or sciences constitutes the major course. If, however, a student pursues a program of business courses, we strongly suggest that he take such subjects as merchandising, advertising, and finance, besides the usual courses in economics, business law, and accounting.

Only recently, some colleges and universities have added courses in real estate. Some of them constitute a wide enough range to provide a major subject toward a degree. In other cases, they are relatively isolated courses that can be included in the student's overall program. In any event, we recommend strongly that anyone with even a slight notion to enter the real-estate field avail himself of such courses, if for no other reason than to test his interests. If he decides to pursue realty as a career, then, of course, he should take as intensive a program in real estate as the college offers. But this is not to say that one should ignore the liberal arts or general courses in government, economics, and other social sciences. In many business situations it is far more important to be well-versed in these subjects than merely to be expert in the techniques of one's own occupation. As we examine the various types of brokerage, we shall see how social sciences, languages, the arts, and science can be helpful in the direct advancement of a real-estate career.

Then there is another way to get a preparatory education—in a business school. Most major cities have one or more of these. And while they give no degrees as such, they usually offer programs that are designed to prepare men and women of all ages for various business careers. Some are more specialized; for example, one in New York City concentrates only on real estate and insurance, while several others prepare students for work as accountants, advertising executives, merchandisers, and the like. Admittedly, business schools with relatively short courses appeal most to those in occupations where a qualifying state examination is required. They offer what we have come to call "cram courses."

True, these courses do not have the breadth of higher education, but they fill an important need. Even the mature man or woman with some business experience in a given occupation can gain much from a concentrated course in the techniques and regulations of their field. Many of the tests these schools use are actual state examinations from past years; how a candidate does on such an exam indicates pretty accurately how he or she is likely to do on the official test. Other schools devise their quizzes primarily to assess their own teaching success. But we know at least one school whose exam is said to be more exacting than the state test.

The requirement by state laws that candidates for broker's licenses have a minimum of practical experience as salesmen or traders is sensible, too. It may be true in individual cases that a person can pass the examination after doing no more than take specialized courses, and can still eventually embark on a successful realty career. But once a broker is licensed, his customers should be able to rely on him for complete service; it is unlikely that mere passage of an examination will equip him for this. Practical experience under the guidance of a broker, on the other hand, supplements his schooling adequately. A broker also benefits immensely from actual sales experience. We should hate to think of the income he would lose without it. Suppose, for lack of experience a broker clearly fails to give a customer all of the advice and service to which he is entitled. This is a customer who will probably take his business elsewhere.

That little Main Street store—with gold lettering on the show window and framed pictures of inviting houses behind it—is an important fixture in the life of the town. The men and women sitting at the three or four desks inside are the liaison between the folks on Elm Street whose home is up for sale and new arrivals from another town who are looking for a comfortable place to live. It would be surprising, wouldn't it, if word had not spread from Elm Street to Park Drive, Jefferson Road, and beyond that the cozy-looking, two-story colonial at 63 Elm is for sale? It probably has. If word of mouth failed to make this news known, then an ad in the local paper most likely did the trick.

Many houses have been sold directly by word of mouth and newspaper advertisements, and the practice should not be disparaged. But the fact remains that residential real-estate brokers make up the largest part of the industry—this is true certainly in numbers and probably in the dollar volume of the business they transact. Moreover, no other type of property goes to the hearts and emotions of buyers and sellers more than the family homestead. Consequently, the residential broker is more than a commercial middleman. He is advisor, diplomat, and friend as well.

The predominance of home selling within the real-estate industry can be judged by observing the activities at a typical convention of the National Association of Real Estate Boards, which is the parent organization of the 1,500 local real-estate boards to which a substantial number of brokers in each community belong. When some 7,000 delegates from all parts of the United States and Canada gather at their annual convention, a good three-quarters of their meetings are taken up by discussions of the market in new and re-sale homes, financing of residential sales, and other topics that deal directly or indirectly with the problems of bringing buyer and seller together in the transfer of a private house. Let us, therefore, examine this phase of brokerage in the light of the work itself, the career opportunities it offers, and the necessary preparation for it.

There are, essentially, three basic functions that constitute the total service that a residential broker renders. The first is to find so-called listings. These are houses put up for sale by their owners, which are known as listings because a seller is said to list his house with one or more brokers. The next is to compile and maintain a roster of prospects, the people who have indicated that they are interested in buying a house. The third is that of negotiating the sale and arranging the details—the contract, mortgage, title search, and title closing—that lead to the consummation of the deal.

Listings are obtained in several ways. Some come in by letter or telephone from owners who wish to sell. Others are solicited by contacting owners, word of whose intention to sell has reached the broker through his social or business connections. Still more are solicited by following up newspaper advertisements placed directly by owners who did not originally use a broker. In addition, some communities have multiple-listing systems, whereby brokers who belong to the network share the listings any one of them obtains.

Creating an inventory of listings—the broker's merchandise—calls for resourceful salesmanship. Not every home owner is readily disposed to sell his property with the aid of brokerage. Some are reluctant to part with the commission. Others fear that an inconsiderate broker will barge in on their home life with the most unlikely prospects. Another group is afraid that brokers want merely to clinch a deal and will ally themselves with the prospective buyer, and together will try to persuade the seller to lower his terms. To overcome these misgivings calls for a patient and thorough sales campaign. When a broker calls on an owner who has placed an advertisement in the paper directly, he knows he is talking to a seller who prefers to avoid brokerage, since it is highly unlikely that any home owner does not know about the existence of brokers. His sales objective, therefore, is to convince the owner of the benefits of using brokerage.

An even more challenging sales job is required to

get an exclusive listing. There are two types of exclusives, though their exact definition varies from state to state. First there is exclusive brokerage. This means that the broker who gets such a listing is the only realty man authorized to show and sell the house. Thus, his commission is wholly protected unless the owner sells the house through his own efforts. The other kind of exclusive is known as exclusive agency. This arrangement makes the broker absolutely the sole agent through whom the house can be sold. Even if the owner sells the house to his brother-in-law, whom the broker has never even met, the broker is still entitled to the commission as exclusive agent. Either type of exclusive listing is of obvious advantage to a realty man.

Each also has advantages for the home seller, but he must first be convinced of it. Most home owners are inclined to feel that the greater the number of brokers who have the house listed for sale, the more likelihood there is of a prompt sale. There is some merit to this view, but there are many things to be said for exclusives, too. For one thing, a broker will expend more effort and money to sell a house when he knows that after his efforts and money are spent, there is no danger that a competitor will snap the deal away from him. Moreover, the home owner is assured that the broker will intrude on his privacy only when he has a likely prospect with him. When a house is up for sale with many brokers, each realty man who has it listed will bring almost every potential customer, no matter how unlikely, to the house to make certain that should that customer sometime decide to buy it, there will be no question about which broker showed him the property first. For the home owner this means many unnecessary disruptions of family life while sightseers with little serious intention to buy romp from room to room. Exclusive listings also usually have time limits so that, if the agent fails to make a sale, the owner can try another broker or several others. This possibility also spurs on the broker to do his best to make a sale.

The process of compiling a roster of prospective home buyers takes considerable skill. It is not enough to have the gold lettering on the window to identify the store front as a realty office. True, some passers-by will drop in just because they see the sign, but their patronage is not enough to keep a broker in business. He must use ingenuity to attract others. One of the accepted methods is through newspaper advertising and, in smaller communities, through radio commercials as well. Brokers use these media in many ways. One is to insert an ad that lets people know about your firm. This type of advertising serves two purposes. It lets prospective home buyers know that a given agency is one place where they can begin their search. It also lets prospective sellers know that it is a place to list their houses with if they want to sell. The other advertising method involves newspaper notices announcing that this or that house is for sale. These are calculated to attract home seekers who are looking for just such a place.

Strangely enough, though, customers rarely end up buying the particular house whose description in an advertisement first lured them to a broker's office. It is obviously up to the broker, therefore, to keep the customer interested in looking at other houses after he has rejected the one he specifically came to see. This calls for both salesmanship and a wide variety of good listings which, in turn, are also obtained through salesmanship. Knowing which houses to advertise and which to show to any given customer, and in what order, is a skill an agent must develop if he is to be successful. There is no surer way to lose a customer than by persistently showing him houses that are unsuitable. And there is no better way to gain a customer's faith than by demonstrating that any house he is shown is at least reasonably well suited to his needs.

Advertising, of course, is the most common form of getting listings and customers. But a broker with ingenuity goes far beyond this. He utilizes his social contacts as well as his business, civic, and club affiliations. In certain situations he seeks speaking or teaching engagements or devises attractive literature, which he has circularized through the community. He may also retain a publicity man who places stories about the agency in local newspapers or magazines or who solicits invitations for the broker to contribute articles of his own. The resourcefulness the broker shows in bringing his agency's name before the public will result in additional listings and greater patronage from home seekers.

Once the broker has brought a seller and a prospective purchaser together and they have reached the point of showing some interest in making a deal, the realty man has to fall back on another form of salesmanship. Only rarely will buyer and seller agree completely on all terms right away. More often, their interests will conflict. The seller wants more money than the buyer is willing to pay. There are other terms about which the principals may disagree, such as the date of occupancy, the inclusion of certain household items in the price, and the like. Some of these can be straightened out at the time the contract is made, but there are some that are so much a part of the sale itself that there can be no deal until they are settled. It is here that a broker's skill is put to the test. He must try to convince the seller to give a little ground without making him feel that he is being talked into defeat, and he must likewise urge the buyer to better his terms without making it sound like a high-pressure sales pitch. If the two parties agree and a contract is made, the broker may also have to arrange the mortgage financing in some cases. He may even have to order the title search and arrange for the closing, at which the deed is conveyed, though in most cases the principals' lawyers take care of these details for their clients.

From this brief description of the job, it should be evident that the residential broker needs patience and a kind of sales talent that is quite unlike that used in a deal between businessmen. After all, he is helping one family to buy and another to sell a possession that is very personal. He may have to tell an owner to lower his price to a realistic level without casting aspersions on his home. And any experienced residential realty man will tell you that it takes a large measure of patience and insight when one deals with families at what is an important crossroads in their lives.

This is one field in which the real-estate man does not usually need an extensive education. Many have been eminently successful with little more than a high-school diploma. It is far more important that a residential broker be gregarious, personable, and willing to take an interest in the peculiar family problems that will be revealed to him by his various customers. Let's look at some of them. One family knows full well that their house will not bring more than $18,000, but they want to keep up with some friends who recently sold their home for $20,000. Another family—this one buyers rather than sellers—must have the approval of a well-to-do relative; and it is important when the house they want is being shown to this relative for approval, that no mention is made of the dry-wall construction, because he would never give his blessing to anything but a plastered house. And then there is the almost standard problem of the family that goes house-hunting with a mother-in-law, who comes along to make certain that the guest room will suit her.

Another frequent need is for a broker to tactfully handle two clashing personalities. Many times buyer and seller are not actually too far apart in their terms, but they refuse to budge and bridge the small remaining gap simply because they react strongly against each other. Perhaps the buyer's children are running, unrestrained by their parents, through the neatly kept rooms of a house that childless sellers still fondly regard as their own. Or an innately distrustful buyer or seller betrays his suspicions to a degree that mars every bargaining session despite the sincerity of all others present.

Let us, then, trace the progress of a young man who chooses as his career a residential brokerage business in a medium-sized community. It begins when the job applicant has completed his education. If he is personally acquainted with a local real-estate broker, he should pay him a visit to talk about a job as a salesman. His friend may have a vacant desk for him or he may know of a competitor who can use young talent. If the beginner has no personal contacts, he will do well to pay a visit to the local real-estate board and have a talk with the executive officer, often a paid employee, or with one of the elected officers who is actively engaged in the realty business. They may have leads for him. If this method is unproductive, he can look in the local realty trade publication, if the community is large enough to have one. And, finally, there are want-ads in the daily newspapers and, of course, there are also employment agencies. If the applicant finds no pertinent ads in the paper, it may be worth his while to place one of his own, offering his services.

Remember, however, that these impersonal approaches are of value mainly in large communities, notably the suburbs of major cities, where personal contact with all the brokers is virtually impossible. We must assume, for the sake of this discussion, that a future realty man is making his choice of a place to settle for one personal reason or another. If he is starting out in the residential field, the chances are that he will look for his first job in his home town or, if this is a large city, in one of its suburbs. There is no practical reason why he would go to some small town, far away from home and all family ties or acquaintances, to look for a residential salesman's job in a real-estate office. The only time to do this is when the beginner wants to locate in a rapidly growing community, such as some of the cities that occasionally spring up around a new type of industry or defense installation. It is likely that a person interested in a real-estate career has at some time or other shown this interest by dropping in on a local broker to see how he works. If his schooling included any real-estate courses, he has also probably come in contact with somebody in the field. We can thus assume that it is possible for almost anyone to make at least one satisfactory connection to help in launching a career.

A well-organized résumé is always an asset, and we recommend that every young applicant repair to his typewriter to draw up one. (We might add here that knowing how to type is of decided importance to the beginner. Until he reaches the stage where he merits the services of a secretary, he will probably have to handle his own correspondence and in some instances even add typewritten riders to printed contracts.) But we will also concede that at this early stage of a career, a résumé is little more than a personal calling card. At best, it shows the applicant's place and date of birth and his education. However, in cases where someone enters the real-estate field after years spent in another occupation, a résumé showing such experience is helpful. Because the realty broker deals with clients in all

walks of life, any experience he has had in other occupations will probably come in handy on some future
occasion.

To enter the residential real-estate business as a salesman, one should own an automobile. This is one of the
few commercial fields in which even an apprentice has
to make an investment. We would like to be able to say
that any old jalopy will do, but such is not the case.
Unfortunately for the young salesman's pocketbook,
he should own either a new car or a used one of recent
vintage that is in excellent condition, both mechanically
and in appearance. It need not be an expensive make;
indeed, it is better to have one of the less flashy brands,
if he is going to be dealing with average people. Perhaps in very exclusive neighborhoods the broker or
salesman with a luxury car may have a bit of an edge,
but even here it is not expected of him. Under ordinary
conditions, a real-estate salesman should have a neatly
kept, mechanically sound, four-door sedan.

It is not unreasonable to assume that many young
men and women about to enter business already own
suitable cars. But if they do not and if they lack the
funds with which to buy an automobile, even on a time-
payment basis, they may be able to work out an arrangement whereby the prospective employer will help
them buy or rent a car. Some realty brokers will even
permit reliable employees to use their cars, especially if
they own more than one. A final note about cars: The
sensible realty man will choose an automobile that is
relatively economical to operate; and he will drive
with the utmost care, especially since he is likely to be
diverted at times by the chatter of customers whose
conversation he cannot afford to ignore.

Once the young trainee has begun his job, there are
many ways in which he can learn more about his work.

Thoughtful brokers will often take a junior salesman along when they negotiate new listings and allow him to attend contract sessions. They will also make their current listings available to him so that he can take customers on house-hunting jaunts independently. But they will always stand ready to take over if it appears that a sale is in danger of going on the rocks unless a skilled hand takes the wheel. A trainee will soon learn the technique of handling customers. He will learn, for instance, that he should do more listening than talking until he has a firm grasp of what a prospective buyer is looking for. He will learn when humor is in order and when not, when to be glib, and when to be plain spoken, He will learn to judge when his customer is showing signs of fatigue and confusion and is likely to start reacting negatively to any house he sees from this point on. He will learn to be increasingly selective in the properties he shows to any one customer and to acquire skill in showing them in the most advantageous order. He will learn how to make and space his appointments with home owners to be sure that he and his customers do not barge into an awkward reception, stand baffled in front of a tightly locked, deserted house, or discover too late that the house has been sold to someone else without the salesman's knowing about it. He will also learn how to control conversations between buyer and seller during early visits so that the two principals will not become alienated before he has a chance to create a bond between them.

Just how a salesman, or a broker for that matter, goes about these things is a matter of personal technique. Suffice it to say here that in one way or another a salesman has to be fully receptive to the problems of both buyers and sellers. Any arrangement he makes to gain access to a house he wants to show is up to him. This may mean calling the seller to see if a visit at a particular time will be convenient. It may mean keeping an extra key in the broker's office when the owner is away, or hiding a key in a secure place on the property. But a customer must never be taken to a house without knowing what will confront him—a locked door with nobody around to unlock it, a vicious dog, or an owner who is ill or asleep.

Practice also varies in the matter of discussing price or terms in general. But a salesman should always talk these things over with each party separately. He should never let them become embroiled in negotiations that may get out of his control. Some salesmen shuttle with offers and counter-offers between a parked car containing his customers and the house of the seller. Others prefer to negotiate with the customer back at the office and pass on his offer to the owner afterward. These are techniques a young salesman will probably pick up from his employer or develop by combining the best features of the methods used by several employers or even competitors. In any event, the apprenticeship of a salesman is a healthy and fruitful period.

Whether it is financially fruitful also depends on his own ability and the amount of activity in his employer's office. There is little that a salesman can do if due to location, personalities, or reputation, the broker who employs him fails to get his share of the area's real-estate business. In such a situation, a young salesman can do one of two things—look around for another position, or become the sparkplug by which a lagging business is revitalized. The latter course will probably give him a good chance at a future partnership. In the meantime, however, a salesman is dependent partly on the business volume of his employer and partly on his own talents. Normally, he is not paid a salary, and only rarely will he be given a drawing account against future commissions. Since commissions can only be charged by a licensed broker under most state laws, it is the employer who receives payment for the deals concluded by the salesman. How much of each commission is passed along to the salesman as his share is determined by individual agreement. It usually varies between 25 and 35 per cent of the total commission. It must be remembered that the employing broker bears the cost of all office overhead and the salesman has virtually no expenses beyond the upkeep of his car.

Even a 25 per cent cut of the commission will give an enterprising young salesman a fairly good start. For years, the standard commission for the sale of a private house has been 5 per cent of the sales price. (Lately, it has risen to 6 per cent and more in some parts of the country.) In the sale of a $20,000 home, therefore, the broker's commission is $1,000. If the deal was actually made by the salesman, his share of the commission will usually be from $250 to $350. A minimum of two such sales a month should keep a young trainee from pleading poverty. Moreover, a progressive employer will pay his salesman an additional small fraction of a commission—say, 5 to 10 per cent—if the salesman originally got the listing or was the first to deal with a buyer who ultimately wound up the deal with the broker.

It is true, of course, that many areas do not have enough houses worth $20,000 or more to produce $1,000 commissions with great regularity. Fortunately, human nature and sociological trends have compensated for that. Areas in which low-priced houses —worth from $8,000 to $15,000—predominate are also the areas in which there is the largest turnover of properties. Thus, a broker in such a locality is more likely to earn a greater number of $500 commissions instead. And then there are the exclusive neighborhoods, where the sale of a $60,000 house brings a

$3,000 commission, of which the successful salesman can expect to earn about $750. If there are fewer sales of this calibre, the larger commissions make up for the difference.

In all honesty, we must also mention here that some salesmen occasionally find it advisable to cut their commissions, though this practice is thoroughly frowned upon by professional associations. Most often this happens when buyer and seller are only a few dollars apart but neither will yield another cent. In such a case, the salesman can bridge the gap by cutting his commission, and thus clinch the deal. Without express permission from his employer, a salesman can reduce only that portion of the commission due him, for he must not compromise his employer's position. In fact, some brokers instruct their salesmen never to cut commissions under any circumstances. In other offices, a broker may, after consultation, agree to such a cut and may even offer to absorb a part of the cut himself.

In the course of a salesman's work, he may find that his agency engages in brokerage other than residential sales. Depending on its location and the nature of the community as well as the personal interests of the broker, the agency may occasionally sell vacant land, apartment houses, commercial or industrial properties, or act as a mortgage broker. Generally, these specialized deals are handled by the owner of the business and do not provide any benefits to a salesman save those of being affiliated with an active agency. In a typical situation, a salesman sells only private houses, unless he has occasion once in a while to negotiate the rental of a home or an apartment. But if he has his eyes wide open, he can learn much about other phases of brokerage, which will stand him in good stead later in his real-estate career. A broad-minded broker will not deprive his salesmen of a chance to learn something constructive about other parts of the business.

Some realty agencies also act as insurance brokers because a real-estate deal so often entails some insurance coverage. When a person acquires property, he usually wants insurance on it. Unless he insists on obtaining this from his regular insurance broker, he can normally be sold on letting the real-estate broker handle it. In this situation, realty brokers earn additional commissions, either by giving desk space to an affiliated insurance man or by acting as their own insurance agent.

Many real-estate brokers also own and operate properties of their own or take an occasional partnership position in a building venture. Often, these interests arise out of a situation in which the broker finds it advantageous not to try to find a purchaser for a given property but instead to buy an equity or a mortgage position himself. (If a man buys a $20,000 house for $5,000 down, he then has a $5,000 equity and the lender has a $15,000 mortgage position.) Such activities do not concern the salesman directly, but he can observe and learn from them. What is more, he may find that his employer is so engrossed in special deals that the bulk of the residential brokerage is left to the sales force, with the obvious result that the salesmen have little competition from their employer in the realm of home sales.

In due time, the young salesman will complete the minimum requirements for taking his state's examination and getting his own broker's license. Whether he takes this step, however, depends somewhat on his relationship with the broker who employs him. There are brokers who will not have other brokers operating in their offices. They want only salesmen so that there will not be competition for full commissions. If this is the case, the salesman must first decide whether to strike out on his own as a broker, to seek an affiliation in an agency where there is no ban on brokers, or to continue to work for his present employer. If the current employment situation is profitable and pleasant enough, he may prefer to forego his advancement to broker's status. In some states he can take the examination and put his license in "cold storage" with the state; thus, he preserves his relationship with his employer and assures himself of a broker's license if he finds it desirable later to pick it up.

This may seem like a pointless course to follow, but not when one considers the peculiar situations that can arise. It is true that as a broker he can operate for himself and keep all of the commissions he earns. But he must also cope with the overhead of running his own agency. If he becomes an active broker in an area where his employer dominates the realty scene to the exclusion of nearly all others, his independence may gain him little besides professional sovereignty. He will possibly be far better off—financially and in terms of security— to remain a salesman and hope eventually to attain executive status or a share in his employer's investment opportunities. In a more competitive area, however, he may find a real-estate agency in which he can work as a licensed broker without being obliged to share in the overhead. In other words, he operates much as a salesman except that his share of commissions is larger. If he completes the sale of a $20,000 house, he will share equally in the $1,000 commission with the owner of the agency. Of course, if he is in business for himself, the commission will be all his, but he must also pay the expenses of running the agency. When working for another broker, he shares the commissions with his employer in place of contributing to the overhead in proportion to his use of the facilities.

Deciding what path to take depends heavily on the individual situation, as it does in any line of work. We do not propose to solve this problem but merely to point out the possibilities open to a real-estate man who is a broker. However, we do advise any aspiring realty man to get a broker's license on becoming eligible. No matter how tempting his position as a salesman is at the moment, there may come an opportunity to make a particularly good deal outside the residential field. If he is a salesman, he has no choice but to let the agency he works for act as the broker, thus losing not only a large part of the commission but also much of the credit the transaction would have earned him in professional circles. If he is a broker in his own right, he can demand a larger share of the profits and will publicly get full credit for handling the deal. If he has established his own agency, the profits are also entirely his—after meeting expenses, of course. In all fairness to brokers, however, we should add this: If a salesman who gets 25 per cent of the commissions he brings in makes an unusually profitable transaction, the broker who employs him is likely to reward him with a bonus or perhaps a financial interest in the deal.

Before we leave the residential brokerage field, let us take a brief look at a fairly new part of the business—the sales agent at a new housing development. Essentially a product of the post-war era, this type of residential brokerage is still in an evolutionary stage; and it may turn out to be a good way for young men to enter the field on the ground floor. Let us look at it from that point of view.

When the demand for new housing became urgent

immediately after World War II, home builders who had previously constructed just a few homes at a time turned to a new type of venture. In some areas of the country we call it a development, elsewhere it is known as a subdivision or a tract. In any event, a development builder begins his operation by purchasing or taking an option on a tract of land sufficient for, say, a hundred homes. On the most accessible corner of this tract he builds a few model houses, which are typical of the hundred he plans to erect. He furnishes the models and then invites the public to inspect them, hoping that a hundred families will find one of them attractive enough to buy.

One of the characteristics of development building is that to make a profit on the whole project a builder must calculate exactly the cost of acquiring and improving the land, of erecting the houses, and of selling them. From experience, early developers learned that brokers' commissions were adding far too much to their overall costs. As a result, developers decided to set up their own sales forces. Today, full-time salesmen are stationed at model houses, and part-time salesmen usually help out on week ends, when larger crowds are expected at model sites. And while the part-timers are usually not expected to follow a sale through to the contract stage, the full-time salesman is responsible for the entire process, though the builder and his lawyer supervise these activities. For these services, builders pay either salaries plus commissions, straight commissions, or straight salaries, depending on local custom and the best way to sell houses on the most economical terms. For many developers, this system has worked rather well.

But there are many others who feel that their sales should be handled by a firm of specialists. Real-estate brokers are clearly such specialists. The earliest arrangements made by developers were with local realty agencies that took on the selling job. They hired salesmen specifically for duty at the model houses, retained lawyers for devising standard contract forms and conducting the contract sessions, planned promotional campaigns (in coöperation with advertising and publicity men), and handled the entire merchandising task for developers. Meanwhile, their brokerage business in resale houses continued on the old basis.

Some agencies are still doing all this, particularly in areas where new developments are not abundant enough to warrant exclusive attention to them. But in other locales, especially the rapidly growing suburbs of large cities, many brokers soon came to realize that acting as sales agents for subdivisions is a profitable and full-time business. Today, we have many such agents, the more successful of which serve dozens of large developers in their areas. Once they began to specialize in handling new-home colonies, they also found that there were other services they could profitably render to the tract builders. They could help developers locate and acquire land for new projects and arrange the financing with lending institutions. Some even found it worthwhile to make investments in their clients' building ventures.

Today, sales agents for housing developments appear to be a permanent part of the real-estate scene. A few of the most forward-looking agents are now even working on ways in which to handle new-home merchandising on a national basis; for instance, they help builders in Florida sell their houses all over the country to people contemplating retirement or employment in that state. Because this field is so new, it offers interesting career opportunities with a growth potential that is limited only by the future prospects of large-scale housing—prospects that look bright in many sections of the nation.

This is one of the fields in which a young man can get started with little more than an average education—high school is enough—and a conviction that he can sell. After all, it is essentially a showroom job. A good way to start is to scan the home section or real-estate pages of a local newspaper to find those home subdivisions that appear to be large and active. If an ad does not give the name of the sales agent, this indicates that the builder is doing his own merchandising; therefore, an applicant has to call on the builder to inquire if he could use another salesman. An ambitious man or one who cannot afford to leave his present employment because of family obligations can look for part-time employment as a week-end salesman to get his feet wet. Unless he contemplates a switch to the building business, however, he may find it limiting to work directly for the developer. If he plans to concentrate on real-estate selling, he will probably do better by following up those advertisements that show a sales agent at work. Again, the applicant should offer his services on a full-time or part-time basis, as he sees fit.

His earnings will come in any of several ways. He may be paid a given amount of money for each deposit from a customer who ultimately buys, he may receive a straight salary, or he may get a combination of both. If he is paid a commission, it will most likely be rather modest at first—$50 a house perhaps. Some sales agents pay this commission when a customer signs a contract to buy a house; others do not pay all of it until title to the house is passed sometime later. That $50 may not sound terribly enticing, but remember that the per-house commission paid a sales agent is not comparable to the full commissions paid on resales of existing homes. Moreover, the sales agent in development selling has not only more volume but also the exclusive right to sell at any tract where he is appointed agent.

No sales agency is so large that its principals could overlook a salesman with a highly successful record. Nor are competing agencies likely to be unaware of the talents of an outstanding performer. Consequently, the chances are excellent that a resourceful, energetic salesman will soon find himself either gaining promotions within his own organization—such as supervisory responsibility for several tracts—or getting good offers from a competing agency. If he thinks that his selling ability is too great to be wasted on employers, he may find it worthwhile to open his own agency and reap the financial benefits of a business in which many sideline activities offer opportunities for profit.

Once a realty man has passed the salesman stage, it is difficult to estimate his income potential. Much depends on his resourcefulness, personality, and perseverance. There is no standard salary for a salesman who has been promoted to a supervisory capacity with jurisdiction over several subdivisions or who has taken a hand in finding land for a builder or arranging mortgage financing for him. It is even harder to find a yardstick to measure the income of an agent who has gone into business for himself. There are some in the New York metropolitan area and other large centers of housing activity who have become exceedingly prosperous since the war. There also are some who have merely scraped by. But for those who are inventive enough and prepared to extend the scope of their activities beyond the local housing scene—possibly to establish national markets for houses in one area or prefabricated houses for delivery anywhere—this is a pioneer industry with great promise of financial returns.

One other aspect of residential brokerage remains. That is the rental market. This is most active in or near large cities. Essentially, it is not much different from the residential-sales field except when it comes to commissions. In its original form, rental-apartment brokerage came into play when the owner of an apartment house sought a tenant for vacant premises. In recent years, however, owners have been able to do reasonably well without the use of brokers in leasing existing apartments —mainly because of the housing shortage that followed World War II. Especially in New York State, where rent-controlled apartments are snapped up by applicants on long waiting lists, there appears to be little need for the services of leasing brokers.

But another specialty has evolved that is very much akin to the function of the sales agent at housing developments. It is the renting agent who takes care of newly built apartment houses. Like the agent at private-home tracts, the renting agent signs up tenants before the building is completed, using either floor plans or model suites. Also like the development agent is the sales agent at coöperative apartment projects.

Brokers who act as renting or sales agents at apartment houses usually operate on a predetermined scale of commissions that varies with the length of lease or level of sales price. Here, as in new-home sales, certain real-estate brokers have come to be specialists. Employment in such agencies should be sought in much the same way as one applies for a job with a sales agent for private homes.

CHAPTER III

Commercial Brokerage

A soupy drizzle made New York's Third Avenue look just about one block long, though it is one of the city's longest thoroughfares. For the moment, the broad avenue had the same oppressive appearance that it had shed only a year before, when the steel structure along which elevated trains rumbled at five-minute intervals still cast its heavy shadow. In one ancient saloon, even the "Bar and Grill" sign, with the "G" extinguished in the dusty neon tube, seemed as morose as the old dog that had flopped on the stoop, and was too lazy to get up and out of the rain.

The gloved hand of a smartly dressed man covered the dirty enamel "Push" sign and the door gave way, letting him in along with a gust of damp air that momentarily diluted the odor of cheap rye, beer, and the grease on the short-order grill. The man took a place at the bar. His shined shoes on the brass rail contrasted noticeably with those on both sides of him. It was obvious that he was not part of the establishment's typical clientele.

The bartender shuffled toward him with obvious displeasure. "You here again?" he asked.

"Yes, I thought I'd talk to you about—"

"What'll you have?"

"A beer, I guess."

The barkeeper shuffled to the beer tap, rinsed a glass perfunctorily under the water faucet, and held it to the beer tap. He shuffled back and put the glass down in front of the customer, who proceeded to nurse the foamy brew for about ten minutes. When the bartender saw that only foam was left, he returned lazily.

"Say, I wonder if I could talk with you just a few minutes," the customer said.

"Another beer?" The bartender was clearly not interested in conversation.

"All right, I'll have another."

The refill came more quickly this time, and so did the bartender's words. "I told you once, my brother don't want to sell, so stop wasting your time," he growled, and slapped the glass down in front of the man.

"But what about you?" the customer asked, looking for an opening.

The bartender hesitated. "I don't know," he answered at last. "I got this place up in the country, you know. Some day I mean to move up there for good." With that, however, he got snappish again, saying, "Anyway, my brother ain't selling. Go see him if you want to."

When he shuffled away again, the customer, convinced that there was no point in sticking around, shoved his half-filled glass aside and got ready to leave. He paused for a moment, fishing around in his pocket for the folder of business cards that identified him with the real-estate firm of which he was vice-president. Then, figuring that he would only antagonize the bartender with the card, he turned and walked out into the gloomy night.

This was his tenth futile visit to the saloon. He had spent many hours trying to convince the man he had just talked to and his brother, who took over during the day, that they could do well for themselves by selling their little three-story building, with the bar on the ground floor and a few dingy apartments above. The real-estate broker needed their property to complete a blockfront for some clients who planned to erect an office building on it. The bar and grill—which brought in enough to support the two brothers—was situated right in the middle of that blockfront. Thus it was impossible to build around it, as one might have if the property had been on a corner.

At last, though, the broker ingeniously worked out a complicated but practical deal with the two bar owners. The night partner, long inclined to seek the greener pastures of Vermont, sold him a half interest in the parcel. Then he got the daytime partner to exchange his half interest for an adjoining piece of land the builders owned in the block. Simultaneously, he leased that parcel back to the builders for a long term. The exchange agreement also provided that the bar owner could open a cocktail lounge in the new office building under a lease that gave the builder the right to reacquire that space, which, in this case, he ultimately did. The final result was an exchange and a lease of land. Today, a gleaming, glass-and-aluminum skyscraper stands on the site. Does the deal sound complicated? Not to an experienced real-estate broker who deals in large urban properties. While the transaction showed considerable ingenuity, it has many of the characteristics of deals that are handled regularly by realty brokers whose business consists primarily of income-producing properties.

In essence, brokers in this category are not-too-distant cousins of the men and women who handle the residential sales described earlier. The commercial-sales field is most active in and near the large cities. Further, it is also a field of considerable specialization. If a brokerage concern of this sort does not restrict itself to deals in a particular category of properties, the chances are that the individuals in the firm are specialists. Thus, we may have an agency in which some men deal primarily in office buildings, others in store properties, while still others are active only in industrial structures. One of the main differences between the residential broker and his colleague in the commercial-sales field is that in dealing in far more costly property, the commercial broker must be able to negotiate with greater agility.

Moreover, the values that he deals with are more elusive than in the residential field. If the owners of a house at 63 Elm Street put a given value on their property, there is little flexibility in the price beyond the personal give-and-take between seller and buyer. With income-producing properties, on the other hand, there is considerable flexibility, based on the variety of financing methods, the type of ownership, and other factors. Ultimately, the value of an income property is determined by the yield that an investment in it will produce. Consequently, if there are ways to increase the yield— through ingenious financing, leasebacks, and the like— various values can be placed on the property when it is looked at from different points of view.

Obviously, then, the commercial broker is concerned with more than land, brick, and mortar. He must understand income potential. But he must also be well versed in the subject of taxation, because tax considerations are playing an ever increasing role in the decisions made by professional real-estate owners and traders. Moreover, he must comprehend the motivations behind real-estate deals. In residential real estate, these are simple. One family seeks to move elsewhere and therefore lists its home for sale. Another family needs a particular type of house in a particular area and is therefore disposed to buy. In commercial realty, however, the motivations are far more complex. They may be tax considerations. They may be business strategy in which an owner finds it advantageous to sell his property and lease it back, thus remaining in the premises and at the same time freeing some of his capital. They may merely reflect an economic prediction that a certain type of building or a certain neighborhood will become more or less profitable than some other kind. In any case, the commercial sales broker must be able to recognize these motivations both in handling the property for the seller and in finding a suitable purchaser for it.

Not all commercial brokerage involves multimillion-dollar transactions. The same principles apply to a one-story building with three stores in it. Indeed, in smaller communities and rural areas such deals dominate the picture. What is more, outside large cities, this type of commercial brokerage is part of the business conducted by the same agencies that handle residential sales. It is only in the more populous areas—those where business life is very active—that the functions of the residential broker and those of the commercial broker are completely distinct and separate. And what are some of the commercial fields? They include office buildings, apartment houses, hotels and motels, downtown store buildings and large shopping centers on the edge of town, individual factories and industrial parks, warehouses, garages, and virtually any land or structures which somebody can use profitably. Farm brokerage, for instance, is an important business by itself.

Though, as we said before, a commercial realty deal need not involve millions, it is obvious that the majority of them do involve sums far in excess of the price of a one-family home. And, of course, commercial properties are not traded as often or as easily as houses. Clearly, then, a broker who handles income properties works far longer than his residential colleague to put a deal together. But his commission is also far larger. Even so, there are complications. The broker with that type of business spends most of his time on research,

maintaining and enlarging professional contacts, negotiating with potential clients and customers, and—
never forget it—making numerous false starts. Large
deals rarely are simple. They do not always involve
merely one buyer and one seller. They may entail three-
way or even four-way exchanges among various parties.
In the land assemblage described earlier, for example,
failure to bring the bar owner around to selling would
have cancelled out the broker's successful deals with
other owners on the block, which took a year's hard
work.

This is a phase of the realty profession in which even
the brightest novices must grow gradually. We can only
offer a brief guide on how this can be done. And we
start by cautioning that this is one field in which scholastic background is of considerable importance. Indeed,
here is a career for which we recommend the greatest
degree of educational preparation that you can afford
to get—either before going into business or while already professionally engaged. There are several courses
to follow. One is a broad program in the social sciences,
which will prepare an able broker for judging sociological, political, and economic trends that affect the real-
estate industry. He should know—and preferably he
should know before anyone else—why a particular section of the country or a city will grow or decline as a
manufacturing or management center; how much rent
certain classes will pay for living accommodations and
what types of accommodations they seek; and what the
government is likely to do with regard to taxation, tar-
iffs, or fiscal and business controls.

Here is a fictitious example. The owners of a downtown office building are offering it for sale. The majority of its tenants happen to be importers of certain for-

eign-made specialties. A broker who senses, because of
his education in the social sciences, that the government
is headed for a higher tariff policy can predict that many
of the tenants in the building will be adversely affected
and that some may even go out of business. Consequently, he can outsmart his competitors by not even
offering the property to investors who depend on the
building's secure tenancy. Instead, he will try to interest
a company that needs a building of this size for its own
occupancy and is geared to take only limited space at
the beginning with the prospect of absorbing the remainder as it becomes vacant.

In addition to a background in social-science studies,
we recommend a program of business studies—preferably a postgraduate degree of the type available at the
Harvard School of Business. Such training will give the
future realty man considerable insight into the motivations that govern the concerns with which he must deal.
This is important in all kinds of commercial brokerage,
but it applies most to those brokers who intend to specialize in industrial property. While most brokers have
occasion sometime in their careers to sell industrial
property, this part of the profession is generally a specialty—and a highly regarded one, too. Within the
framework of the National Association of Real Estate
Boards is the Society of Industrial Realtors, whose members are especially capable of advising manufacturers
on the proper selection of plants and helping others sell
plants they no longer wish to own or occupy.

But to give proper advice, a broker must be thoroughly familiar with such concepts as horizontal and
vertical business organization, separation of management functions, etc. To attain such knowledge requires
not only practical experience, but a thorough scholastic
background obtained in a business school, preferably of

college status. Also, there are always realty courses given at short-term business schools.

It does not matter much where a man who is seeking a career in commercial brokerage first starts employment, because his initial berth will serve as a vantage point from which he can survey the field. Once he has an idea of the types of properties that he wishes to deal in permanently, he can look for the agencies that are most likely to offer him this opportunity. Having been active somewhere in the realty business already, he is in a good position to know what brokers engage in the commercial dealings that he is interested in.

Having had some experience, the applicant is able to present his prospective employers with a more attractive résumé. And this is one phase of the business where a well-prepared résumé is of value. It should state, besides statistical data such as birth and personal background, what education and the degrees the applicant has. This information should be followed by a full description of the positions he has held, indicating not only the duties entrusted to him but also brief details of the deals he has negotiated to date. Normally, we would recommend that a résumé begin with the last position held and work backward chronologically. This is the general procedure with résumés in most businesses. But for a position in a large brokerage concern, the reverse often has advantages. By presenting his experience in true chronology, the applicant gives his prospective employer a better view of how his talents have developed. By the very nature of the business, it is likely that he will have progressed from relatively simple deals to more complex ones. And it is precisely this sort of growth that an employer looks for in choosing a new associate.

There is no firm pattern that governs the progress of a

young broker in the commercial field. One thing is certain, however; he is not likely to make his best strides until after he has obtained his broker's license. As a salesman, his scope is limited and so is his income. Once he is licensed, he is not only in a position to see his big deals through and reap full credit for them but he is usually accorded added recognition within the agency, too. At least one large realty firm in New York, for example, promotes every member of the staff to a vice-presidency as soon as they get their license. The prestige that such standing commands also brings professional recognition, which leads to more attractive deals. A broker, especially a vice-president of his agency, is in a much better position to step into a business situation and offer to solve the client's real-estate problems than is a mere salesman, though we do not wish to imply that a salesman cannot handle matters capably if he has the initiative to pursue good leads.

Once a young broker has become affiliated with a large agency, he is pretty much on his own. The agency may train him by assigning him to the management division and other departments before turning him loose in the market. During this training period, he will most likely get a modest salary. But if his past experience indicates he is ready, he will begin immediately by working on his own deals. In some agencies, he will get a drawing account to sustain him financially until his first transactions begin to bear fruit. In others, he will have to rely on his own resources. Whatever the case, his income will depend entirely on his own production. The chief assistance he obtains from his parent concern is the free use of its facilities—free, that is, if you disregard the fact that he must share his commissions with his employer on a fifty-fifty basis, to pay his share of the business overhead. How much he earns in commercial brokerage depends—as it does in the residential field—on the reputation of his agency, on his own ability to create and pursue transactions, and on the realty market in general.

Unlike the residential brokerage business, however, commercial deals are not initiated by people calling up a broker to list a forty-story skyscraper for sale. True, this sometimes happens. But more often than not a broker has to find these deals for himself. There is a reason for this. In commercial real estate, it is folly for an owner to "peddle his deal around town"—as they say in the trade. If the owner of a substantial property enlists the aid of every broker in town to sell his building, he creates the impression that it is not a very desirable property. (Somehow this psychology does not apply to private houses.) This happens because the same potential purchaser may have the property offered to him by a succession of brokers. The inevitable conclusion is that if the property is worth the asking price, its owner would not have to list it with every broker in town to sell it. Obviously, this means that the astute realty owner will be coy about offering his holdings for sale—so coy, in fact, that he will let word of his intentions leak out as if by accident. It is not uncommon for a broker in the commercial field to tell a customer, "I think the owner could be convinced to sell if he had a ready purchaser." This is a somewhat tarnished truth. Through his channels of information the broker has good reason to believe that the owner is not only prepared but eager to sell under the right conditions.

This should make it clear that the commercial realty business is no place for someone who wants to sit at a desk and wait for a client to walk in and ask to list his property. Rather it is a profession in which the successful practitioner will follow up all leads—word of mouth, newspaper stories and advertisements, comparable transactions, and the rest. For example, word that an owner is seeking a new mortgage for his building may be the tip-off to an alert broker that this owner is preparing to offer his property for sale with attractive financing. Having made this deduction before his competitors, the alert broker can bring a customer and close the deal before the competition even knows that it is open.

Because success in this phase of the realty business depends so much on personal ingenuity and aggressiveness, it is a field that offers as much opportunity to the lone wolf as it does to the organization man. While it is an advantage, on the one hand, to be affiliated with a large, well-organized agency into which flow some of the juiciest business tips, it can be equally beneficial, on the other, to be in business for oneself if one enjoys the freedom of a one-man realty office.

What about income? Because of the vast variety of deals and the complex collateral arrangements they often entail, there is no certain way of pinning down earnings. Suffice it to say that the broker in the sale of a $100,000 property—whether it is an apartment house, office building, or whatever—earns an average commission of $5,000. Ordinarily, there is a sliding scale in most metropolitan areas, and as the amount involved in a deal goes up, the commission percentage goes down. The rates for brokerage in vacant land are sometimes higher, and land sales constitute a highly profitable field that attracts many active brokers. Often, of course, brokers have to split commissions. This happens when they act as co-brokers in putting a deal together, either because circumstances so dictate or because they agree in advance that together they have a far greater chance of success than alone. But regardless of how a commercial broker operates—in his own business, in partnership, or for an agency—he is in a highly lucrative profession—one in which millions have been made. It must be remembered, however, that the largest transactions tend to take place in the big cities. Still, a commercial-realty broker in a smaller community can look forward to a satisfying career, especially if he can reduce competition by attaining a position of pre-eminence.

There is another occupation in the commercial-brokerage business that is also largely confined to the larger cities—the leasing broker. Often this type of brokerage is pursued in conjunction with a general brokerage or management business. But some brokers have come to specialize exclusively in leasing.

The leasing broker earns his commissions by bringing together the owner of a property with someone who wants to rent space in it. In most cases, the commission is paid by the owner. The space in which the leasing broker deals is in office buildings, in stores, in loft buildings, in industrial plants, or in warehouses. Again, some brokers specialize in only one category. Most commercial space is rented on the basis of square footage, though store space usually is leased by the front foot—that is, the amount of street frontage. A typical office lease specifies that the tenant pays, say, $5.00 a square foot per year. An office of 6,000 square feet, therefore, costs the tenant $30,000 a year. Under a ten-year lease this means an aggregate rental of $300,000. Commissions to brokers on this type of deal are usually calculated on a sliding scale—5 per cent on the first year's rental, 2½ per cent on the second year's rental, 2 per cent on the next eight years' rental, etc. The commission on the above lease would be $7,050. It will readily be seen that this can be a highly profitable business.

Then there are the many subsidiary deals that a good lease can generate. For example, if a broker convinces a company to lease space in one building before its lease on another has expired, he may also obtain the listing for subleasing the space the company will vacate. Even if the first lease has expired, the mere fact that the tenant is moving automatically creates another vacancy, which the leasing broker will then attempt to fill. Of course, this is another instance in which being alert counts. For a very short time, the broker who makes a lease may be the only one who knows that his customer's old space is becoming vacant by virtue of the deal. If he can find a new tenant for it before the competition hears of it, he may not only earn another commission but, in chain reaction, will have still another block of space to fill.

One of the prime attributes of the leasing broker is the instinct of a detective. In Sherlock Holmes fashion, he must be able to deduce from various apparently unrelated data that a given space is opening up or that a particular company is getting ready to move. How does he find this out? By reading the newspaper advertise ments, for one thing. If he is systematic in his approach, he will make a record of newspaper accounts and other reports that give him some clue of when certain business leases are due to expire. Putting this information into so-called future files, he will get in touch with the landlords and tenants concerned before these leases expire; that way, he may end up with two commissions— one for helping the tenant to find new space and the other for helping the landlord find a new tenant. A resourceful leasing broker also keeps in close contact with what a detective would call informers—furniture movers, furniture supply houses, and the like. If their friendship is cultivated, they will let a broker know in advance when they are called upon to move one of their clients.

A good leasing broker must be an adroit salesman who is able to recognize quickly the needs of a customer as well as the vital features of a given block of space. By being able to demonstrate convincingly how that particular space fits the needs of that particular customer, he will close a deal that competing brokers, with less salesmanship, would fail at.

Another area of commercial leasing is that of exclusively representing landlords as renting agents. This part of the business, which is by nature confined to the larger cities, appeals to many because it affords relatively certain income. It is parallel to the job of the sales agent at home developments or the renting agent at an apartment house. The leasing agent of a new office building is charged with getting tenants for all of the space. In most cases, his fee is a set proportion of the regular leasing commission. In commercial leasing it is customary for exclusive agents for buildings to pay commissions to outside brokers who bring customers. In most instances, leasing agents for major buildings are brokerage concerns with general practices as well. For this reason, they have access to extensive information about what major corporations are in the market for new space. Another benefit of being named leasing agent by the owner of an office building is that the agent has a preferred standing as a candidate for the management contract, too. (This is a subject that we will go into in the following chapter.)

Again we must emphasize that commercial leasing and particularly the role of the renting agent are confined to large cities. In small towns, when an owner wants to find a tenant for commercial space, he can always turn to a local brokerage concern, which in all likelihood handles residential sales, land, and all the other phases of realty as well. But usually small-town landlords need not even seek the help of a broker; business leaders in small communities know who the owners of the buildings are and vice versa, and they much prefer to negotiate among themselves.

Where commercial leasing is an active part of the local realty scene, we suggest that the newcomer to the business first get a job as a salesman. Here he can learn the various techniques of locating space, developing a roster of potential customers, and negotiating leases up to the point of signing. To obtain such a job, a young man should apply to as many agencies as he can conveniently contact, preferably with a résumé showing his background. His educational background will be examined only to the extent that a future employer may wish to use this means as a method of elimination.

A good salesman in the rental field need not hold a college degree to qualify. But we must emphasize that when a broker deals with large business concerns that have intricate corporate problems along with production and management considerations, education in business and social sciences is of incalculable value. Not only does it enable him to confer with his customers on their own terms, but it gives him the kind of perspective with which he can help the customer realistically solve his business problems—those relating to commercial space, anyway. After serving the required period of time as a salesman, the realty man is ready to take the brokerage examination. Whether he chooses to remain affiliated with his employer or strike out on his own depends largely on his personal situation and the prospects of the local market.

While we are on the subject, let us take a moment to discuss how much money it takes to start a real-estate agency—any kind of agency. Essentially, it takes only as much as it costs to pay advance rent on a modest office, to buy a desk and chairs and a few other pieces of equipment, and for a telephone. As we noted earlier, this is why the young broker who now dominates the market on the peninsula south of San Francisco chose to become a realty man. Still, it is not advisable to start an agency on a shoestring. An agent should not operate out of quarters so remote that even his most devoted followers have trouble finding him.

If he is opening up a business in a small town, he can probably do better by taking a storefront office, even if it is small, on an active business street in the best section of town. If he does not plan to handle residential brokerage—many residential clients walk in off the street—then he does not need a storefront office. A comfortable location on an upper floor of a store or office building will be sufficient. If the broker is looking primarily for residential work, he should choose a prominent store location in a residential part of town.

In the larger cities, he must decide almost from the start whether he will seek residential or commercial business. If he inclines toward residential work, he should open a storefront office in that part of town where he expects to get the largest number of his listings. If he has plans for commercial work only in a large city, his best bet is one of the respectable office buildings in the central business district. Just how elaborately he should decorate his office depends on his budget and his tastes. Only when dealing with the largest of commercial clients is it at all necessary to have an impressive office. A simple, neat, business-like office is normally quite adequate. If after becoming successful, a broker wishes to go in for professional decorating and penthouse locations, that is his own affair.

By and large, we would say that a broker can go into business for himself with less than $1,000, provided he is prepared to get along without a secretary. The chances are that he will make progress because to get a license he must have a good deal of professional experience behind him. The contacts and the know-how he acquired during his apprenticeship are bound to assure him of at least a decent chance to survive in business for himself. Then, too, he may want to team up with one or more partners, in which case the expenses will be shared; though the overhead in this situation is larger, it is not proportionately so, and, of course, the income potential is also multiplied.

We would not presume to advise any young man or woman whether they should ultimately go into business independently or work for someone else. But we urge anyone considering a career in realty to remember that freedom of action is important for a successful real-estate career. Only when a broker is able to seize upon an unusual business situation without hesitating can he make the kind of strides that lead to phenomenal success and income. Clearly, a person seeking secure, salaried employment has no place in a field where earnings are made through commissions that are not paid until deals are completed. In any event, if a man enters realty brokerage in quest of commission income, he is not likely to be frightened by the risks of going into business for himself.

However, many affiliations with large agencies are more lucrative than independent status. Some real-estate firms enjoy such fine national or local reputations that any broker in their employ cannot help but benefit from them. In such instances, a broker has chances at giant transactions that he could never hope for if he were running his own agency. When a broker has an arrangement of that sort, he probably would do considerably better by holding onto it than by starting out for himself.

Regardless of whether a broker works independently or as a member of an agency, his resourcefulness, perseverance, salesmanship, and negotiating ability finally will detemine how far he climbs up the ladder to success.

CHAPTER IV

Realty Management

The telephone jangled at the side of the young man in shirt sleeves who sat at his desk absorbed in a cost sheet that from a distance might have been taken for a half-finished crossword puzzle. His eyes remained on the figures, his pencil marking the spot where he left off as he reached for the receiver and answered matter-of-factly.

"This is Carlsen at the Beverly Arms," said the voice on the other end. "Looks like the boiler's out and the auxiliary won't do in weather like this."

The young man took one look at the snow-covered roofs outside his office window, nodded to himself, and said, "I'll be right over." He hung up and reached for his jacket in almost the same motion.

Less than an hour later he walked into the Beverly Arms, and made his way straight to the basement, where, he knew, Carlsen, the superintendent, was doing his best to provide heat for some one hundred families. The boiler room was alive with people. Carlsen had taken no chances. He had called the oil supplier and an electrician right after he notified the management office, in the hope that a few skilled hands could get the boiler going again. They had accomplished something; they had traced the trouble to a hopelessly burned-out armature in the firing gun that, under normal conditions, vaporized the oil and sprayed it, ignited, into the combustion chamber.

Informed of this situation, the young man—officially, the building manager—knew he had an important decision to make, and quickly. The owner of the building was in Europe and could not be reached soon enough to be of any assistance. Besides, as a part-time real-estate investor, the owner was actually less qualified than any of those present to make the most prudent decision.

The question at hand was: Should the electrician replace the armature at a cost of less than a hundred dollars, even though the rest of the machine might not last out the season? Or should they invest in a new gun, which would cost nearly ten times as much but would guarantee trouble-free operation for years to come? Although the managing agent had similar responsibility for a dozen buildings of this size, he recalled, as he was trained to do, that this oil burner was original equipment in the Beverly Arms and was over ten years old. He knew enough about these burners to realize that, even with a new armature, more trouble lay ahead, possibly that very winter.

"Let's get a new burner in before nightfall," he told the superintendent. Hurrying into the latter's apartment, he asked for a telephone directory. There was no time to get a lot of cost estimates, but still he did not want to order a new burner at any cost, even in an emergency. As an experienced building manager, the young man had at his fingertips the names of several reliable heating contractors who would make on-the-spot bids. After a few calls, he made a deal with one of them, and before nightfall the radiators at the Beverly Arms were warm again.

In this instance, the professional manager discharged a dual responsibility capably and conscientiously. In representing the owner of the Beverly Arms, he made a quick, intelligent decision that, though not the cheapest solution, was calculated to save the owner money in the long run. Nor did he waste money, because despite the need for quick action, he shopped around for the best bargain. At the same time, he also lived up to his obligation to the tenants in the Beverly Arms to provide them with essential services—in this case, heat and comfort on a cold winter night.

A manager's life is not always as hectic as pictured in this anecdote. Nor is every property managed by an agent who does not own it. But it is important to examine the several possible careers that grow out of owning property for income purposes. Some are closely tied to the brokerage business; others are more closely allied with the role of investor or developer. But regardless of the specific role in which the manager is cast, it is worthwhile to become familiar, first, with his duties and, second, with the type of individual who is best suited by temperament and training to devote the largest part of his business life to property management.

Without much imagination, one can readily see that a major property—an apartment house, an office building or a shopping center, among others—cannot be operated without some sort of professional administration, whether by the owner or by an agent he retains. The job begins even before a building is completed. During the end of the construction period, the managing agent, who usually acts as renting agent as well, lays out a program for attracting tenants. While construction of a commercial building—office or shopping —would not normally start without some lease contracts already signed, residential structures are still largely speculative. This means that the managing agent works either with advertising agencies or directly with newspapers and other media to plan and execute an effective merchandising campaign. When prospective tenants come to look at the premises, the manager or his salesman shows them the available apartments and negotiates with them the terms of their leases. And while the rental terms—the amount of rent and the length of the lease—have been determined in advance by the owner or builder, it is usually up to the managing agent to work out minor problems with prospective tenants in such a way that they will sign up.

Once a building is finished and occupied, the manager's job becomes more complex. There are, first of all, routine operations that require attention—collecting rent, keeping books, and such. Another duty, which is usually routine but is occasionally fairly complicated is paying real-estate taxes. Normally, the manager merely has to check these against the known assessed valuation of the property and the local tax rate. However, if the property is reassessed, it is up to him to find out whether a new and higher assessment is in keeping with the valuations of other similar properties. When the tax appears unduly high, it is the manager's obligation to do something about it—at the very least, to inform the owner of the problem. If the owner is not engaged in the actual operation of the building, the manager will have to tangle with city hall himself and get the valuation reviewed to see if it can be reduced. To this end, he may have to retain a lawyer and, ultimately, to make many of the decisions on his own.

Insurance is another responsibility of the managing agent. This in itself is a complex field. Adequate coverage includes not only fire, compensation, water damage, and extended risks, but also liability in the event of injury on the premises and other kinds of damage. It is the manager's duty to be thoroughly familiar with available insurance policies—both in relation to cost and coverage. Although most managers work closely

with insurance agents who help them with these problems, managers are not paid to rely on insurance men
blindly.

Paying wages to the building's staff is another of the
manager's jobs. In a less complex day and age, this
was a simple matter of withdrawing the proper amount
from the bank and parceling it out in those handy little
pay envelopes, but it is hardly a simple task today. Now
the manager has to figure out federal and sometimes
state withholding tax. He has to make deductions for
social security, workmen's compensation, group insurance, and pension plans—all of which have to be accounted for exactly before each employee's take-home
pay is set aside. In other words, bookkeeping for payroll purposes alone involves a maze of records and requires someone who is equal to keeping them in order.

Standard chores out of the way, the manager next
settles down to the problems that occur less regularly.
The tenant in 4D reports the refrigerator out of order,
and the superintendent wants to know whether it should
be repaired or replaced. And if it is to be replaced, where
and at what price should they buy a new one? The door-
man reports that the rubber mats used to protect the
lobby carpet in dirty weather are almost worn out. A
roofing expert says that new roof decking will be needed
within a year or two. An electrician points out that with
the increased use of electrical appliances, rewiring of
the entire building should be considered. And then there
is Mrs. Johnson, in 5B, whose lease expires in two
months and who is preparing a tall list of changes that
she insists on before she will renew it for another three
years.

For the most part, the principles behind managing
an apartment building are the same in running an office
building or a shopping center. But they still have somewhat different and more complex operating require-

ments. In office buildings, space is not as well defined as it is in a residential building. It contains no three-room or four-room units but rather entire floors that can be subdivided in various ways. Thus, the manager has a problem, since a given vacancy will fit the needs of some prospective tenants but not others. This often means shifting some tenants around within the building to create the openings that can be most easily rented.

In an office building, too, the rental terms are less rigid than in an apartment house, since space in the former is leased on a per-square-foot basis. And because office space is usually offered on the market without fixtures or separate rooms, the manager has to work with the tenant to prepare the space for his use. The layout —including new partitions and doors, along with those fixtures that the tenant needs but does not provide for himself—must be written into the lease. In store properties, still different problems arise. In some cases, store tenants provide their own heating and cooling while in others these services are provided by the owner.

It is not the purpose of this chapter to teach the various techniques of property management but rather to tie up its many duties with the kind of background that is helpful, or sometimes necessary, to carry them out successfully. It is easy to see from the rough job description that an efficient property manager is a man who wears many hats. His headgear includes that of the real-estate broker, the maintenance supervisor, the insurance and tax counsellor, the space planner, and the adroit business negotiator. If the manager does his job well, he lifts all responsibility from the shoulders of a building owner, who may well be an absentee investor or possibly even a group of investors known as a syndicate. A good management background is clearly a great advantage to a striving young man in the real-estate investment field. Knowing all the ins and outs of operating buildings efficiently, he may find it highly profitable later in his career to invest some of his own savings, plus funds of friends and associates, in reasonably sure income-producing property. That way, he will not have to be dependent on outside management.

Property managing, like most real-estate careers, does not depend on any specific educational experience, though a college degree and training in a business or realty school are decided assets. Because management is usually the starting point in the training program of large real-estate concerns, a young man just out of college or school will find himself learning this phase of the industry almost as soon as he lands his first job. In other words, an ordinary job application with a medium-to-large realty organization will probably lead to management training if the applicant is accepted. And there is a good reason for this. Training in property management is the best way of becoming acquainted with the realty man's basic commodity—land and structures.

By the very nature of the management field, the activities of the property manager are pretty much confined to his own city and its surrounding area. If his firm has branch offices in other cities, separate management teams have to run the operation in those locations.

Let us assume for the sake of this discussion that a trainee decides to make the management part of real estate his major career. What, then, is his future financial outlook? In most instances, real-estate firms will manage a building for 3 or 4 per cent of the annual rent. In other words, for a building whose tenants pay a total of $50,000 rent a year, a professional manager will charge the owners $1,500 to $2,000 a year for his services. If he is looking after enough properties to justify a staff, he may employ one or more experienced management specialists. Salaries for such people range from $5,000 to $15,000 a year (plus bonuses in some cases), depending on their experience, competence, and the area the business is located in. Some realty companies organize their management divisions under a department head who earns from $10,000 to $25,000 a year. In turn, he has command of a staff that varies in size and income.

Before entering the management field, a young man should take stock of his personality and make certain that it is suited to the life in this field. The main difficulty in the job is that the realty manager serves two masters—the owner of the building and the tenants. True, it is the owner of the property who pays the manager. But the building will not have tenants very long if the manager, as the owner's deputy, throws his weight around to enforce his boss's orders. A newcomer to the management field will soon find out that there are two sides to every argument, and will learn quickly to be an arbiter between the tenants and the owner. This means convincing the landlord that a tenant's position has some justification and at the same time preparing the tenant for the news that his request will not be entirely granted, and for good and understandable reasons.

By and large, the management field does not claim a monopoly on the extroverts of the real-estate industry. Nor is it a bedlam of weird working hours or places. But a good management man must be sufficiently outgoing to keep the property owner happy and still have enough verve left to do the same with the tenants. And while most of his work is done at a desk during the normal working day, there are occasions when he must take his eyes off the clock. For example, drawn-out negotiations with a prospective tenant for space in a building may go on into the night before both parties reach agreement on a lease.

And then there are alterations. In a well-managed office building the job of putting up or taking down partitions for new tenants or revamping the layout of old ones is a task that the building superintendent usually oversees. If everyone has the proper instructions, alterations proceed as a routine operation. But there are times when the premises have to be made ready for the arrival of a major tenant—a situation in which a slip-up could mean the beginning of an unpleasant relationship that might continue for the duration of a ten-year lease. In such rather special cases the manager does himself as well as his client a favor by supervising the operation. This does not mean doing any of the physical work, of course. (In fact, union agreements usually prevent him from lending a hand.) But his presence on the scene and his specialized knowledge will help avoid the kind of mistake that can cause the owner untold embarrassment.

If on occasion this calls for an all-night session, the ambitious management man should be ready—and willing—to stay on the job all night if necessary. It is not often that a building manager has to answer an emergency summons in the middle of the night, but even this happens at times. No matter how good the maintenance and the safety precautions in a given property, essential equipment has been known to break down at two o'clock in the morning, and for some reason fires, burglaries, and other mishaps are common threats of the night. When they occur, the managing agent is certain to be called out of bed to attend to the situation personally. In fact, his home telephone is likely to be the one listed as the building's night-emergency line.

Labor relations is another phase of property management with which he has to deal from time to time. However, he is not often called upon to set policies, because these are usually determined either by the owner of the building or the head of the management concern. And in the larger cities building-service unions negotiate industry-wide contracts by which each property manager must abide. The skill with which the management man handles his labor problem is measured by the number of disputes among members of the building's staff he can settle himself and the degree to which he can harness their loyalty to the ownership.

For the young man who has mastered the art of property management, many well-paying related careers are open. Let us remember that building management is a specialty found most frequently in the medium to large cities and far less in the small communities. While it is true that many income-producing properties are owned by investors who get their main income elsewhere, the professional real-estate manager has a greater opportunity in ownership than they do because he knows the best ways to develop the productivity of a property to the fullest. To acquire this ability, a young man interested in this specialty would do well to serve an apprenticeship in a real-estate firm of a major city. Depending on the requirements of local realty concerns, a young man planning a small-town real-estate career can apply for a trainee's job on the strength of his educational background, preferably including a college degree. Here, in the course of a few years, he will get acquainted with many of the subtleties of professional management before striking out on a career of realty investment and management.

Let us, therefore, take a close look at the possible careers in real-estate investment operation, and syndication. Ever since the passing of the rather primitive days when every man built his own abode and the shop where he plied his trade, people have more and more been living and working in rented quarters. This has led to a

socio-economic system in which space—land or structural—has become a commodity; its maintenance, as a
result, is a service for which people are prepared to pay.
Consequently, the ownership and development of income-producing real estate has evolved as a full-fledged
business—one that beckons many young realty executives. Here is a career in which the true extrovert, the
self-starter, the originator, and the individualist can
have a field day. This is where some of the nation's outstanding fortunes have been made. Today, the stock of
such ownership enterprises is being traded on the country's leading stock exchanges and over-the-counter
markets. Among these realty firms are such giants as
Webb & Knapp Inc., Tishman Realty & Construction
Company, and the Kratter Corporation. Then there
are the many real-estate empires built by the syndicators, including such masters of the trade as Lawrence
A. Wien, J. M. Tenney, Louis J. Glickman and the principals in the Lifton-Hechler-Weingrow Enterprises, to
name just a few. And while there are only a handful of
such giants, there is a legion of smaller operators who
limit themselves, in the country, to local areas and, in
large cities, to individual neighborhoods. By and large,
however, the principles of their operations are much the
same and differ mostly in scope. And the encouraging
aspect of it is that the potentialities of the field are very
large.

It would be foolhardy to ignore the fact that getting
a substantial start in an ownership career requires money
—lots of it at times. And let us not accept too blindly
the blandishments of those published and rumored reports of millions that have been made with an initial investment of $1,000. They may well be true, but let no
one put his hard-earned $1,000 on the line and expect
to end up with a real-estate empire, unless he has some
solid experience in property management and other

phases of the industry—not to mention ability, drive, and luck. More often than not, the chance to make that killing comes about during management or brokerage activity when an ownership opportunity arises that the young go-getting speculator can safely cope with.

Assuming, therefore, that a young man has received some training in property management and possibly in sales and brokerage, he can then keep on the alert for a suitable investment opportunity. This may come in various ways. Say that an owner for whom he manages a modest piece of property indicates that he plans to dispose of it; or a seller lists a for-sale property with a broker. The young realty man who has accumulated sufficient knowledge and experience to see the income potential of the property if it is properly managed, may find that this is the time to make his first investment. The chances are that he will have to settle for a relatively small acquisition on this maiden venture, since he will probably have to depend solely on his own savings. To entice friends and other potential investors into a deal without first proving himself may defeat his purpose—that is, to build up a following through outside faith in his ability.

To make a sound investment, a young realty man must use a variety of talents almost immediately. The first to come into play is the ability to negotiate wisely with the seller—on the basis of an objective analysis of the property that shows whether the income potential claimed by the seller is really there. This is where sound management training can spell the difference between success and failure. For example, a man with such experience is able to examine a building's records to determine whether the costs projected by the seller are in line with a realistic operating budget. Have such items as heating fuel, payroll, insurance, maintenance, and repairs been correctly estimated? Will the current leases be renewed at the same rentals, or have the neighborhood or the structure's usable characteristics and facilities changed drastically? Is the equipment providing heat and electrical power serviceable for future requirements or are improvements needed? If so, how much will their cost cut into income? Does the property offer a favorable depreciation picture in relation to the taxes on the income it is expected to produce? These are but a few questions that one must be able to answer with assurance before embarking on a real-estate investment venture.

Once the property has been acquired, the young investor must be able to put his income-producing ideas into effect. This is where the young man's ability as a self-starter and innovator will make itself felt. The simplest thing to do is just let the building go on as it did under the former owner. But usually when an investor acquires property, he has a plan for improvement in mind. Now that he owns it he has to put this plan into action. This may mean starting work on physical improvements—such as installing air conditioning, redecorating a lobby, or converting old operator-controlled elevators to automatic ones. It may mean charging higher rentals based on future modernization. This may also involve negotiations to move a tenant from one part of the building into another in order to clear the best space for a future occupant who is prepared to pay higher rent. If it is a store property, the new owner may have plans to acquire a neighboring piece of land for construction of a parking lot to increase the property's overall utility and hence its value. These things do not happen by themselves. And if the new owner habitually puts things off, he may start his improvements too late to gain the planned advantage. Consequently, this is clearly a field that belongs to the man who will act sensibly and effectively the moment he has the opportunity.

The ability to present a logical, realistic picture of his plans is another asset for the young realty investor. The first person he must get on his side is the lender who will give him the mortgage necessary for making the deal. Investment programs have been known to fail because their sponsors were unable to convince a lending institution of their merits, even though these programs had merits. It is obvious, therefore, that a young man planning to pursue a career in real-estate investment must be able to present his ideas clearly and persuasively. This is true also of the investor who has proved his ability to invest for himself and has reached the stage where he is ready to take along outside investors on his ventures. Here his job of presenting a convincing—and at all times truthful—picture of his project is even more difficult. While the mortgage lender who makes a loan has at least an implied guarantee that it will be repaid with interest (a prime obligation of the property owners), partners who participate as investors have no such assurance. They must be prepared to put their money on the line with no guarantee of anything but a fair chance of making a profit. The accuracy with which this risk is calculated by the professional investor determines his future success.

Considering the risks involved—and let us not forget that each new piece of property represents a new risk regardless of the success of former investments—what are the financial rewards to which a young man can look in this phase of the industry? To state it simply, his income depends almost entirely on the return on the investment. But unlike an investment in stocks or other securities, where he has no direct control over management, the real-estate investor's returns depend directly on his ability to convert the property's potential into income through efficient and imaginative management. The range of return on real-estate investments is an extremely wide one. Large shares in sound properties often yield little more than 7 per cent. Other properties, owned through a delicately balanced arrangement of mortgages and leases that provide a large measure of financial leverage, have been known to return 15 per cent and more to the investor. And there is no way of even estimating the capital appreciation that can be attained by shrewd investment.

Take the example of those men who plowed their money into the barren sand along the lonely highway that passes through the sleepy resort town of Cocoa, Florida. Today, these investors watch with something more than satisfaction as the satellite-bearing missiles streak off into the sky from their launching pads at Cape Kennedy, the spit of land that abuts Cocoa. Now, every square foot of that property bears a fantastic price tag, and its owners are hard put to decide whether to reap a quick, large profit by selling their holdings or to build and operate the motels, shopping centers, and housing accommodations that are assured of attractive incomes for years ahead.

There is, of course, a substantial difference between real-estate investment in smaller communities and large, metropolitan centers. In small towns, improved properties are not traded often because their values are not subject to the dramatic changes experienced in the cities. Consequently, the young man with a good management background who establishes himself in a small or medium-sized city must think conservatively. The chances are—and this certainly is true at the out-set of his career—that he cannot make a satisfactory living purely by investing in real estate. Most likely, he will do this in combination with another activity not requiring such large capital, such as brokerage, management, appraising, surveying, and the like.

In big cities, on the other hand, the investment field has considerably more romance, though not necessarily more stability. Because the small-city operator invests only in sound fees (direct ownership of the land and buildings), he seldom becomes involved in the financial acrobatics in which his big-city counterpart must often indulge. His principle is simply to own a sensibly located property, collect rents from the tenants, maintain the building in good operating condition, and profit from the net income after operating expenses.

His brother in the big city, however, can operate on a large scale without buying any real estate as such. His investment may be in a leasehold, which is the right to operate a building that stands on somebody else's land; to do this, he simply pays the owner an annual ground rent. The professional investor may even go one step further and operate the building under an agreement with the owner of the leasehold. In any case, we are not going into the intricacies of this type of deal here. Suffice it to say that through complex arrangements such as this it is possible to "own" a multimillion-dollar skyscraper with a relatively small investment and make a substantial distribution to investors—12 per cent or more—in addition to earning a handsome income from the management of the property.

While we are on the subject of professional realty investing, let us touch briefly on a related topic—taxes. It is no coincidence that many of the more successful people in real-estate investment either have a background in law and accounting as tax specialists themselves or have such an expert on their staffs. Intimate knowledge of the federal and state tax laws is becoming an integral part of real-estate dealing today. There are two reasons for this. One is the possibility that after an Internal Revenue man has reached into the investor's pocket, there may not be enough profit left to justify the risk of owning a property. The other is the modern concept of making money by losing money; that is, profiting from the fact that a building loses in value, as far as taxes go, through depreciation on the books, while in actuality its practical market value and earning capacity remain undiminished. Since under the law one can put down some part of a building's yield as replacement of capital to offset its depreciation (on the books), it is also possible to retain this yield as income without paying taxes on it—simply by putting off the tax until such time as the property is resold for more than its depreciated value.

Tax considerations have also given rise to another strategy in real-estate dealings, known as the sale-and-leaseback transaction. This was considered revolutionary when it was put into use by one or two well-known realty men following World War II. Since then it has become a standard form of transaction. There are many variations of the basic theme of the leaseback, depending on the type of property involved, the nature of the seller-tenant and buyer-landlord relationship, and the specific objectives of the transaction itself.

Here is a simple illustration. A manufacturing concern owns a factory with a mortgage on it. As part of the tax deductions allowed the manufacturer under the law, the company claims as business expenses the real-estate taxes it pays on the factory as well as the interest on the mortgage. By selling the plant to an outsider and leasing it back for use, the manufacturer can now deduct all of the rent he pays to the new owners as a legitimate business expense—much as a merchant deducts the rent he pays for his store. Because the manufacturer's rent is obviously a greater sum than the realty tax and interest combined, the manufacturer has the benefit of a larger deduction from his taxable income. Moreover, by selling the plant he can free the capital he had invested in it for expanding his business or buying new machinery and supplies. For the purchaser of the plant, who now becomes the landlord, the property provides income with an allowable deduction for both depreciation and the real-estate taxes and interest he assumes with the purchase. In addition, he has a reliable tenant whose ability to pay the rent he need not doubt and who is not likely to vacate the premises. And, what is more, he is probably able to buy the factory at an attractive price because the seller-tenant does not wish to incur a taxable capital gain from the sale. In other words, the entire transaction is tailor-made for both seller and buyer when it comes to taxes.

We illustrate this fairly simple example of a lease-back deal to show how the creative mind of a man who is thoroughly familiar with accounting and tax practices can think up a lucrative transaction out of whole cloth. We say out of whole cloth because there is no immediate deal in prospect before he provides buyer and seller with a motive for making it. The manufacturer is normally not a potential seller because he has no intention of moving out of his factory. And the investor has no reason for buying the factory because there is nothing he can do with manufacturing space.

This should solve to some extent the dilemma of the young man whose plan is to attend a college or university where specific real-estate courses are not available. The question he might ask himself is: What education program can I follow to prepare myself for a real-estate career if I cannot, or choose not to, restrict my curriculum to realty courses? Our answer is: A program of law, accounting, government, and business management. With a solid background in any or all of these, a man can readily enter the real-estate field through one of several doors. He can become a trainee in a realty firm that handles property management. He can go to work for a broker as a salesman, for with his scholastic background he will have no trouble passing the state examinations for a broker's license after he has served the required apprenticeship. Or he may apply for a position on the staff of a realty investor, real-estate corporation or investment trust.

Even though he has come out of college with no concrete real-estate experience, he will find that a simple résumé will open these doors for him. By stressing his educational background in résumés sent to such concerns he is likely to find them interested in interviewing him because so much emphasis is placed nowadays on training in business management, government, administration, tax accounting, and law. Résumés of this type should be sent first to the publicly held realty corporations; i.e., corporations whose stock is traded on the exchanges or over the counter. A second target for such résumés are the larger and more active professional investors. He can find their names while still in college by scanning the real-estate pages of the major metropolitan newspapers or by subscribing to some of the trade journals of the real-estate industry. Careful study of the realty press will also give an alert student a ready list of concerns whose names appear with some regularity in accounts of major transactions.

Sound training in real-estate management is also a benefit for anyone who does not have the stomach for the tension that goes with the wheeling and dealing that a professional investor must carry on, or who feels that his personality or contacts will not enable him to line up the financial backers he will some day need to expand in the investment field. If any of these limitations apply, he would probably be happier as a salaried employee. Even so, opportunity beckons him, too, once he has absorbed his training in the management division of a real-estate concern.

Two major opportunities stand out in this regard. One of them is as a real-estate executive of a large company that is not directly engaged in the real-estate business. There are many of these, covering almost the entire gamut of manufacturing and mercantile activity. This is a result of the age of specialization in which we are living. Time was when the president of a non-realty company or one of his top-echelon adjutants attended to whatever real-estate dealings were necessary in pursuit of the company's primary business. If the job became too intricate or involved too much of a key employee's time, it was farmed out to a real-estate company for a fee. Today, however, top executives of large concerns are beginning to realize that even their most highly rated men are amateurs in the realty field and that often even outside professionals are too much out of touch with the company's operation to do the job well. What is needed is continuity, which can best be attained by assigning an employee permanently to the real-estate side of the business; even better, of course, is hiring a specialist for the task. To fill this position, a man should have a background in property management at the very least, and, if possible, additional training in brokerage, mortgage financing, and other phases of realty work.

The real-estate specialist in a large corporation has a variety of duties, some concerned with taking care of current property holdings and others with planning for the future. Let's look at a few examples. The company needs a warehouse in a particular location, and it becomes the realty executive's task to find one and then either negotiate to buy it or set up an agreement to lease it; another possibility is to locate a suitable plot of land, buy it, and build a warehouse. Conversely, a company wishes to dispose of a warehouse it no longer needs. Another company needs to lease showroom or store space, expand or consolidate its executive headquarters, or relocate a branch office. In large concerns, this is a matter for high-level planning, which puts the realty executive in charge of it in the top ranks of the corporate hierarchy.

But there are day-to-day realty chores as well. The lease of an office or showroom maintained by a company is about to expire and has to be renegotiated or, as an alternative, another block of space has to be found and leased. Or the heating bills of a major plant have been out of line with what they should be, and corrective measures must be found to operate the plant at peak efficiency. Then, too, there are the routine matters of attending to the mortgage, realty tax, and rent obligations of the company's properties wherever they may be located. So much detail is involved in these tasks that in very large corporations the real-estate executive mainly supervises a staff of juniors, while he gives most of his energies to the major projects of future planning.

Obviously, this is no position to be undertaken without prior experience in a real-estate concern. A young man would be ill-advised to apply to a large company without having first served such an apprenticeship. Once he has this experience, he should cite it in detail when he submits his résumé to a large non-realty company. If he has the spirit of salesmanship, he may even apply to a corporation that has not previously engaged a realty specialist and try to convince its officers that the time has come for them to hire one. The chances are that his starting salary will not exceed $7,500, especially if he is to work under the supervision of an officer who is currently responsible for realty management. But with a show of efficiency and enterprise, this income can grow rapidly.

This is also where schooling in law, accounting, government, and taxes is a great asset. If, for example, the young realty executive of a manufacturing company has the initiative to undertake such studies, he may well develop a plan by which the company can enter a sale-leaseback transaction of the type described earlier. It would be naïve to think that the company's top management men have not thought of this, too, but they may never have carried out their ideas. Just imagine the stature of the young real-estate executive of a large company after he has negotiated a deal by which the company improves its tax position substantially and frees some of its capital for expansion and a better competitive footing. Even one successful deal of this type is likely to place such an executive in contention for one of the company's top management posts, such as a vice presidency. But his opportunities do not stop there. In carrying out his real-estate duties, the young executive will undoubtedly learn much about the primary business of his employer, whether it is manufacturing or one of the mercantile, transportation, or communications fields. Having achieved some stature within the company and exhibited his general business ability, he is then in a position to gradually delegate his real-estate duties to an assistant and work his way into the top shelf of the management cabinet.

The second opportunity for salaried employment in real-estate management lies in the chain-retailing business. This type of work is somewhat akin to the responsibilities described above in connection with the job of the corporate realty executive. It differs from that primarily in that the chief concern of the retail-chain employee is leasing new outlets rather than managing old ones. In this respect, his work is like that of a broker, and thus some training in brokerage is essential. This is a worthwhile specialty to develop, for it will give you a knowledge of far more than pure real estate. For one thing, you will pick up a good deal about market research—that is, about how to appraise a neighborhood to determine whether it will support a store of the company's chain, or how two of the company's stores can best serve a given area without ending up in direct competition. And yet it also involves such solid realty skills as negotiating advantageous store leases.

As far as income in this work is concerned, a starting salary with a medium-sized retail chain will vary from $5,000 to $10,000, and increases are dependent not only on the realty man's ability but also on the growth of the chain itself. Chain concerns in a class with J. C. Penney or F. W. Woolworth, for example, have been known to pay $40,000 to $50,000 to their chief realty executive. Lately, retail companies have been more inclined to build rather than merely lease their own stores. In fact, some have been building entire shopping centers with their own outlets as the focal points. When a concern embarks on a program of that scope, of course, the man at the controls commands a sizable salary, as much as $50,000. But situations of this sort are the exception and not the rule.

A realty executive who develops great skill as a chain-leasing specialist may also choose some day to leave the ranks of salaried employees and go into the real-estate business on his own or as a partner in an agency. He can do this by lining up one or more retail chains as his clients, serving them as he has been serving the company for whom he worked as an employee. By establishing a clientele among chain operators, he should have little trouble finding a comfortable berth in a good real-estate firm if he does not choose to open his own.

If a realty executive holds a position in a company or

chain of national scope, he must be prepared to travel often. True, his trips are usually not as long and tiring as those of a salesman on the road, but they are a necessary and important part of his job. It is almost impossible to describe their pattern, for this varies with each concern. But it stands to reason that the realty officer of a large enterprise must periodically visit, at least briefly, all of the company's locations. On the other hand, when a major out-of-town project is in the works—say, negotiations for a new plant or the opening of a new store— he must be willing to live out of a suitcase for as long as the situation demands. Sometimes, too, an executive of this type will return home from a prolonged series of out-of-town talks to be greeted by the news that some detail of the project has gone awry. This means he has to repack and head out to the airport again.

There is a third choice for the management executive who wants the security of a salary. This is the field of civil service, especially in the federal government, though there are some posts in state and municipal administrations, too. If, however, security is the prime objective, one must realize that there are income limits imposed by the civil-service table of organization. The top policy-making positions in most branches of government are usually appointive, which means getting the job through political activity. By the same token, political appointees must be able to roll with the punches traded in the political arena, which hardly qualifies as job security.

Here, in short, is the situation. One federal agency heavily engaged in real-estate dealings is the U. S. Post Office, which must lease or own the thousands of stations and sub-stations that make up this vast communications network. To operate this real-estate complex, the Post Office has a sizable staff in Washington and elsewhere. Many members of this section are trained, professional realty men whose salaries, dictated by civil-service pay schedules, go as high as $12,000. The major policy decisions are made by an Assistant Postmaster General. He is a political appointee, however, and his tenure depends on his party's hold on the White House as well as his ability to stay in the good graces of those who hand out the jobs. Needless to say, this is not a position for a young man, nor is it one that you apply for with a cordial letter and a résumé. As for the civil-service positions (and there are posts for real-estate experts in many government departments), they have to be applied for through the regular channels of competitive tests.

From this survey of the management field and its related occupations, it should be apparent that there are many routes to success that a young man can choose. Some involve management itself, while others require experience in different realty activities. Some require capital, while others pay big returns without any personal investment except time, talent, and effort. Nor is it necessary for the job applicant to decide on his future course when he settles down behind his first desk. In fact, he will not really know what opportunities lie before him until he becomes engrossed in his work and builds up his business contacts. Indeed, management is a branch of the industry in which a man can readily tack with the prevailing economic winds. He can find good employment when income security is most important and investment capital is scarce, and he can strike out on his own when a promising situation presents itself. Moreover, there is nothing to prevent him from returning to the fold of a large company when that seems advisable—a move he can make by citing his experience as an independent operator.

CHAPTER V

Building

To think that a dumb-waiter—or the lack of one —could have marked the end of a brilliant building career for two generations seems incredible. But it almost happened. Back before World War I, a young lad who was a recent arrival in New York from the Old World was keeping body and soul together by carrying sash weights from a supply pile on the ground to each floor of a new building and installing them in the window frames as the structure rose story by story. Paid on a piecework basis, he earned three to four dollars a week, and those were the days when a $5 bill still rated as a comfortable week's income. Soon the sash-weight installer became discouraged when he realized that as the building grew higher, his trips downstairs and back with more weights consumed so much time that they cut deeply into his piecework income.

Early one morning, the sight of the night watchman leaving for his daytime leisure gave him an idea. "Want to make some more money?" he asked.

"Sure," the watchman answered. "How?"

"Tell you what. You bring me sash weights from the pile, and I'll pay you for every trip you make." The watchman agreed, and before long the sash-weight business became profitable for both of them. They made at least $20 a week between them—an enviable income in those days.

Having found this scheme successful, the young immigrant looked for other short cuts. In due time, by dint of hard work and frugal living, he accumulated

enough money to build something on his own account.
He decided on a brownstone residence in Brooklyn,
where such houses were being built and sold quite successfully. Using the considerable skill he had gained by
observing his employers in the past, the young builder
turned out an attractive house. But when the time came
to sell it, customer after customer turned it down. Not
being familiar with the gracious living that prevailed at
the turn of the century, the builder had neglected to in-
stall a dumb-waiter for carrying meals from the basement kitchen to the dining room upstairs.

The omission nearly ended a promising career in the
construction field. But the young man's dogged deter-
mination to establish a family business for his children
helped him overcome that first failure. He salvaged
what he could from the house and went on to build
many others. In time, he was landlord to hundreds,
and his construction business netted enough to enable
him to support his family comfortably and to send his
son through college. When the boy graduated—as an
engineer—he took over as his father got ready to retire.
Having a dynamic business approach of his own, the
son expanded and streamlined the construction operation by bringing to it financial skill that astounded even
his widely experienced father. Today, theirs is a highly
respected real-estate organization that provides attractive, reasonably priced housing for thousands of New
Yorkers. With the advancing years, the patriarch of the
family has turned over the business entirely to his son.
In time, the former sash-weight worker will see his grand-
son step in to carry on this multimillion-dollar business,
which almost never got started for lack of a dumb-
waiter.

Not all successful careers in the construction business
start so humbly or face an early crisis over a minor er-

ror. While many a builder still goes into business in shirt-sleeve fashion, there are just as many who approach it with an executive slide-rule technique that they acquired in colleges of engineering or business. Then, too, hard-minded thoroughness often pays off. Take, for example, the builder who came across an attractive piece of suburban land that had been turned down by others because it was too far from water lines and sewer connections. As a result, the owner was willing to sell cheaply. Curiosity aroused, the builder tramped over every inch of the land to examine the site. Before long, he came across a manhole cover that was nearly hidden by underbrush and moss. Scraping the growth aside, he discovered the terminal of a water line that even the municipality had never recorded on its maps. Armed with this knowledge, he purchased the unwanted tract at a bargain price, and developed it with a colony of private houses that earned him a handsome profit.

Considering that the value of land—realty's most important staple—is most commonly exploited when something is built on it, the role of the builder certainly looms as an essential one. We are not concerned here with the contractor, the man whose business it is to put brick and mortar together, but rather with the speculative or investment builder. He is the fellow who plans and executes the construction of buildings of all types and sizes with the objective of selling them at a profit or operating them for gain by collecting rent from their tenants. This is a wide field, encompassing the entire range of residential, commercial, and industrial structures, and it offers a wide variety of career opportunities.

Since the term "speculative" implies that the building field involves risks, it follows that it holds little attraction for the man whose ultimate goal is a steady salary. To realize the full income potential of the building industry, one has to be prepared to assume the risks it entails. But this does not mean that one cannot obtain some good basic training, without risk, as an employee in an active building firm. And while we are not going to go into the details of the contracting business, it should be stated here that some of that basic training can be obtained through an apprenticeship with a general contractor. Ideally, however, the properly trained investment builder should also be familiar with the principles of real-estate brokerage, management, appraisal, and other specialties of the industry. He must also know the market value of the land and its rental revenue. All of these are a part of the proficiency he needs if he is to exercise prudent judgment and control over the combined operations that determine the success or failure of a building venture.

But before we analyze the process by which a young man (or possibly even a young woman) charts a career in the building field, it may be well to look at what makes this part of the real-estate business tick. What are its various forms? How does it produce income? What are its pitfalls? What is its future?

The first thing that probably comes to mind when one thinks of construction is the home-building industry. And this is only proper because it is the nation's largest single fabricating industry. It is also, we might add, its most decentralized. While the nation's automobiles and television sets are produced by only a handful of giant manufacturers, the houses in which more than half of its population lives are being built by some 20,-000 separate companies, few of which complete more than twenty homes a year. Most builders are the independent sort. For one thing, they are usually reluctant to become organization men. For another, although each builder's product looks like those of a thousand competitors, he will insist that his is different and mean it. And the chances are that somewhere in its design or construction or in the way it is sold it is distinct.

Herein lies the strength of the home-building industry as a bastion of individualism. Americans may be content to drive cars that have the stereotyped marks of the assembly line, but they are less willing to live in assembly-line houses. To be sure, today there is a good amount of development housing, with homes that were built in assembly-line fashion, but even so, the individual home owner has given his place a distinctive stamp. One of the best examples is Levittown, on Long Island, where Levitt & Sons once erected some 17,000 very similar homes; ten years later, there are few houses in which the owners have not demonstrated their pride of possession by making enough changes to set their homes apart from the rest. Also, the notable increase in prefabricated homes in recent years is due in part to the public's awareness that even a factory-made house can be changed to satisfy individual tastes.

Generally speaking, there are three types of home building in which an attractive career awaits the man with imagination, good taste, judgment, and perserverance. They are custom building, speculative building, and large-tract development building. Let us look at each in turn.

The custom builder warrants the least of our attention because in terms of career opportunities he constitutes the smallest segment of the industry. (Some custom builders are also general contractors, and as such they are not included here since that occupation lies outside the field of real estate proper.) There are, however, some areas of the country—notably, the better suburbs of our big cities—where the custom builder is more prominent. Unlike the contractor, who merely builds a house from plans and specifications supplied by the client's architect, the custom builder comes into the picture at the start of the home-building process: when the housing needs of the family concerned are analyzed and discussed.

He also helps his client look for a suitable building site, relying on his experience and judgment to give advice on what plot is most suitable for a given type of house. Many custom builders believe that some architectural training is a decided asset for their kind of work; some, indeed, are accomplished architects. Yet even those who have no architectural training usually take a hand in drawing the rough outlines of the general plan. But ultimately the design is usually done by an architect, and the builder's only job is to produce the house within the purchaser's budget as set forth in the construction contract. Once construction is under way, the custom builder performs in much the same manner as general contractor, reaping his profit from the margin between the actual cost of the house and the price paid by the client, which is usually about 10 per cent. His skill and judgment is measured by both his profit and the home owner's satisfaction. If his profit is rather limited, so is his risk. He has no investment in the construction project beyond the amount he advances for a very short period toward the purchase of materials and the payroll of his construction crew.

The speculative home builder, on the other hand, takes a greater risk because he invests both in land and construction. The typical speculative builder is a fellow who acquires at his own expense land for one or more houses in a neighborhood where he expects to find a ready market for new dwellings. He then puts up one or two houses along designs he believes to be in demand. As the homes near completion, he offers them for sale at prices calculated to produce a comfortable profit, part of which he will most likely invest in future houses.

Whether or not he can make a profit from each venture depends mainly on his judgment of the residential real-estate market. First, he must select desirable plots and negotiate for their purchase at prices that are in proper ratio to the value of the houses he plans to build. Next, he must choose a building style and a room layout that will be acceptable to the average buyer. And lastly, he must sell the houses at prices that are sufficient to pay for all phases of the construction process, including land acquisition, labor, materials, and financing costs.

This type of speculative building is often good training for the young man on his first construction venture, because the risk is relatively small and so is the initial investment. All that the speculative builder usually has to buy outright is the land, but he can get a start by buying a single plot for anything from a few hundred to a few thousand dollars, depending on the locale. If, in his earlier training, he has learned how to deal with subcontractors, he can start construction with limited funds and wait for a building loan to help him finance the completion of the house. Once he has the structure sufficiently advanced to sell it—just before final finishing and decorating—he can count on the purchaser's deposit to see him through to completion. If his calculations were correct, his margin of profit should be adequate to provide him with a living allowance and enough funds to start another house on an even more solid financial footing.

A home builder who seeks to enlarge his operation with an eye to netting impressive profits must eventually turn to large-tract developing. Within the realm of the home-building industry, this is the form that big business takes. The large-volume developer—perhaps the maturest species of home builder—must commit himself to the purchase of vast acreage. This means that he has to study his market carefully to determine population trends and the economic complexion of residential areas, lest he find himself with a piece of land that will hold hundreds of houses for which there is little or no demand. He also has to be thoroughly familiar with zoning and construction codes, because these determine to a large extent what type of house can be erected on the land he selects.

Once he has acquired his tract, he works with his architect in designing one or more model houses that lend themselves well to the mass production principle. This may seem easier than it really is. The finished product must be attractive and contain the space and amenities demanded by a public that has become more and more selective and whose tastes are constantly changing. The model must also be adaptable to rapid reproduction on an assembly-line basis with a minimum of wasted materials and remnants. And its final cost, together with the cost of land and its improvements, must be calculable to almost the last penny. For those who have examined model houses at developments, this is probably the answer to the question you asked: Why didn't the builder put an extra closet here or a stall shower there? The reason, more often than not, is the necessity to produce the group of houses at a unit cost that, combined with the builder's overhead and profit, will be salable at a predetermined price.

Then there is the builder's task of negotiating for the financing that he needs both to erect the homes and to sell them. If, for example, he plans a colony of a hundred houses to sell for $20,000 each, he must secure mortgage commitments averaging at least $15,000 per house—or a minimum total of $1,500,000 in loans. This, of course, is big business. And, finally, there are the contractual relationships with building-material suppliers, subcontractors, mortgage-lending institutions, and, of course, the home buyers. Here, again, a background in real-estate practice as well as in law and accounting is extremely helpful.

We have cited these problems not to scare the budding young developer but rather to enlighten him. After all, informed authorities tell us that this nation needs more than a million new homes a year merely to accommodate the growing population and to replace obsolete dwelling units. This estimate does not include the demand for homes from families seeking to expand into larger or more luxurious quarters. And in the low-to-medium-price brackets the trend is definitely toward large-volume developing because of its efficiency and relatively low unit costs. This means that opportunity awaits the young builder who is prepared not only to work efficiently but to come up with new methods and new products. In fact, large-scale home building is one of those industries where there is plenty of room for the pioneer. This is true also of home prefabrication, which is nothing more than mass construction in the factory without the concern of finding land on which to build.

With this in mind, how should a young man plan for a career as a home builder? We feel that, like most careers, this one should start in college. It should include a major in structural engineering and training in business administration, law, and accounting. But we must also be candid and admit that of all real-estate opportunities this is the one in which the young man without college training has the best chance of succeeding, for he can get much of the necessary training on the job. But the ranks of the home-building industry are constantly swelling with college graduates—mainly engineers. And there is a good reason for this. Since the margin of profit varies with almost every house that is put up, a builder cannot afford to be forever calling in engineers to solve the grading problem for this plot or that, to help with an occasional drainage problem, or to advise him on the best way to bridge an outsized span for a customer who prefers not to have a wall between the kitchen and the family room when the basic house happens to have one. The more independence he shows in solving these problems with a slide rule and the local building code, the more control he will have over his projects and their return.

This does not mean that the college graduate, the ink still wet on his degree, should attempt to enter the home-building industry, least of all the large development phase of it, without an apprenticeship. If he wants to hasten the day of his independence as a builder, he would do well to hold down some summer-vacation jobs with local home builders before he graduates. But, regardless of any pre-graduation experience, he should spend anywhere from one to three years working for an experienced builder, or for first a builder and then a real-estate broker who deals in new and resale houses. This kind of training will enable him, first of all, to get the feel of a piece of land, to determine whether it lends itself, physically and economically, to residential development, and if so in what price class the houses should be, considering the zoning requirements and the economic status of the neighborhood.

Another field to master during an apprenticeship with a builder is the proper way to purchase materials— buying lumber in advance when the price is favorable, negotiating with subcontractors, and the like. Then there is the construction process itself—the skill of putting a quality house together at the lowest practical unit cost. And, finally, there is the need for tact and skill when it comes to selling the houses and arranging the mortgage financing for the purchasers. For this part of the process, an apprenticeship with a real-estate broker who also acts as a mortgage broker is invaluable.

There is no scholastic way to get this background, nor do home builders run training programs like those in large business concerns. Written applications and résumés are virtually unknown in this field. We suggest that a young man who wants to become a home builder apply for a job with a builder who is active in his area. The applicant should briefly describe his education and then make it clear that he is ready to make himself useful in whatever capacity and at whatever salary are fitting, given the situation.

And once such an arrangement is made, the future builder should invest in a pair or two of coveralls and prepare himself for some good hard work during his apprenticeship. The first year will be the toughest. It will most likely include some time spent as a laborer doing odd jobs at the construction site. But since it was made clear that the newcomer hoped to rise above the manual-labor stage, the intelligent employer will undoubtedly give him more and more opportunities to take on extra responsibilities. If the first job does not work out to his satisfaction, the trainee should be light footed enough to look around for another builder who is better equipped or more favorably inclined to show him the ropes. We might also point out that some of the most successful apprenticeships have wound up with the trainees' being assigned to executive jobs in the building concern.

Once a trainee has absorbed as much as he can from his employer, with no permanent job in the company being in prospect, he would be wise to turn next to a salesman's job with a local real-estate agency. Here is his classroom for the lessons to be learned in dealing with one of the most unpredictable specimens of the human species—the home buyer. He must be led, cajoled,

convinced, flattered, and sometimes even scolded; but
he also must always be accorded the dignity he deserves
as an American about to establish a home in the community. His problems are many indeed at house-buying
time, and he looks to the sales agent for the solutions.
Knowing how to handle the buyer and his problems
will be a valuable piece of equipment in the home builder's mental tool chest. It will enable him to appraise the
market for current buyer preferences, financing
methods, and other related sales techniques.

During the training period, the future home builder
should not look for much more than a subsistence income. Depending on the degree of his usefulness to
his employer, he will earn somewhere between $50 and
$100 a week. But if he considers this in the same light
that a young physician regards his internship, it will
not seem so bad at all. If he develops special skills during the early years, he may even improve his income
while still in training, but this is not the objective. After
all, if the trainee becomes highly proficient at superin-
tending concrete-foundation work, it is a signal for him
to move on to an activity that he has yet to master. This
is a period of life, we might add, of roughing it—of eat-
ing lunch out of a paper bag or lunch box with a ther-
mos bottle, of coming home at night in sore need of
soap and water and maybe even some liniment.

The training period spent with a real-estate agent may
be frustrating in another way. The trainee, who is instrumental in bringing sales almost to completion, has to
sit by while they are tied up by a more experienced
hand. If he is allowed to sit in on contract sessions and
title closings at all, it is only with his promise that he
will keep his mouth shut. And, if he takes full advantage of his training opportunity, he will have to spend
long hours studying the broker's records and files instead of indulging in the more glamorous outside

chores. While his starting salary in a brokerage office will be nominal, perhaps even nonexistent, he does have an opportunity to earn some partial commissions from his seniors by showing houses to customers who eventually buy them.

Once the necessary training has been absorbed, the young home builder is ready to start his first construction project. Through the contacts he has already established, he may be called upon to put up a custom home on a non-speculative basis; that is, building it for a customer who is already committed to buy it. This involves a minimum of invested funds and if carried out efficiently, it will net the novice a modest profit. He may also start, in the manner described earlier, by building one speculative house, selling it, and reinvesting some of the gain in another house. As he gains momentum through good management of his affairs, he should also increase his annual income from a bare subsistence level to a comfortable living. Subsistence income in this case usually takes the form of a salary the builder pays himself at the start as part of his overhead.

As he progresses, his financial needs will enable him to figure out how much of his income he should set aside for his personal use and how much he should reinvest in other building ventures. Once he has accumulated sufficient capital to begin a large-scale development, he should begin casting about for a suitable tract of land. He is ready to launch the development of his site when he has purchased and subdivided the land, negotiated the mortgage financing, and prepared plans for the model house or houses. Here is the beginning of his first big business venture, one in which his income is limited only by his ability to produce and sell good dwelling units in sufficient numbers.

The margin of profit varies widely in development

houses. For example, developers have been known to do well with a 5 per cent profit when they are building low-priced houses in large quantities. This means that a developer who constructs and sells a hundred homes a year at $12,000 each, has an annual income of $60,000. The chances are, however, that he will not undertake a project of this size without partners because of the capital and manpower required. Developers whose production runs into thousands of homes a year can obviously work on an even smaller margin and reap profits in six figures. We can only speculate on what Levitt & Sons' profit was over the five years during which it built the 17,000 inexpensive homes on Long Island or, later, its work on communities of similar size in Pennsylvania and New Jersey.

But the Levitt enterprise is unique. Many builders have done well by creating colonies of homes costing $25,000 and up, where each house is somewhat different from the next. In this type of operation one cannot compute unit costs as accurately as when all the houses are identical. But a builder who specializes in varied houses is likely to find great satisfaction in it and will thus take his chances with this phase of the industry. His financing problems are different and so are his sales methods, his land planning, and nearly every other facet of the developing process. A builder in this group may find that his margin of profit varies with almost every house, but it is still considerably larger than for those who build cheaper homes in greater quantity. Some builders have found that it is best to diversify—to build low-priced houses on a large land subdivision in one place and a group of more expensive houses on a smaller plot at the same time.

And, finally, there is the man with some experience in the industry who decides that he would rather devote his time to more artistic pursuits. He will undoubtedly go into the practice of constructing from one to five homes at a time, each a distinctive, highly artistic residence. And while he cannot expect to reap the profits of the large-scale developer, once his reputation is established he can earn a very handsome living and enjoy the satisfaction of the creative life according to his own leanings.

It is important to emphasize here that the real-estate man who devotes his life to home building must be a man who does not require the comfort of a sheltered routine. Once he has achieved a sound financial footing, he can open an office in a downtown area, but the chances are that he will start with his home as his headquarters. Still, even when he has opened an office, the bulk of his working time will be spent at the construction site. No two days will be alike. Just as he has gotten into the swing of coping with foundation work, this phase of the job is finished and he must concentrate on another process. And while he may enjoy his visits to lending institutions or conferences with suppliers and sales brokers, he must face the fact that this is only one day's activity and that the next morning he will be back out amid piles of lumber and freshly dug mounds of earth. And just as he begins to enjoy the comfort of the construction shack and the attentions of the waitress in the local lunch wagon, he will find that the project is completed and he must move on to another location. But this variety is the very thing on which the genuine home builder thrives. He is not cut out for the life behind a desk in a real-estate office or mortgage institution. He seeks the outdoors and feels happiest when he is moving about.

There are two exceptions to this in the home-building field. One is the manufacturer of prefabricated houses. The other is the head of a large, corporate home-building enterprise. There is little need to deal here with the prefabricator, who is essentially a manufacturer and only in the most general sense a real-estate man. But we should take a look at some of the characteristics of the corporate home builder because his is a breed that is just beginning to come into its own. To date, some examples of this part of the real-estate industry are All-State Properties, Lefcourt Realty, and, most recently, the aforementioned Levitt & Sons. Most of them operate on similar principles. They are large-scale home developers who, because of the larger resources of a publicly held corporation, can range much further in their operations. Their stocks are traded on the exchanges or over the counter. With the capital raised through stock and bond issues they are able to work on several large developments at a time, developments which may be separated by hundreds and sometimes thousands of miles.

In this type of operation, a knowledge of home construction combined with managerial talent is equipment for a rewarding career in a rapidly growing industry. We venture to say that if the home-building field is to show any signs of consolidating, it will be in the direction of this type of corporate enterprise. Because the field is relatively new, it is difficult to estimate the income potential of the young recruit. More than likely, he will earn about the same salary as the young employee of a local builder. But the advancement opportunities are far greater. They may involve travel or frequent relocation of one's home as the ˉcompany completes projects in various parts of the country. But after some years in the field, successful executives are often assigned to the home office—the managerial base of operations. Because of today's tax laws, corporate home-building enterprises sometimes offer their young executives stock options, which eventually give them a share in the ownership and profits of the venture.

The life of a speculative builder outside the private housing field is much like that of the home developer. The main difference is the merchandise—apartment houses, office skyscrapers, shopping centers, factories, motels, and such. The project has to be reasonable from its beginnings so that the risk is a sensibly calculated one. In this respect, the commercial-building field differs substantially from home construction. There is hardly a house built that cannot be sold to someone— usually at a profit but if need be at a break-even point or at a slight loss. This is not so with other kinds of construction. Therefore, the speculative builder must be a man of many talents, a man of vision and judgment, and a vigorous salesman. Let us take the various types of structures one by one; then let us examine the career possibilities in each.

The speculative builder of apartment houses must first judge the rental market to determine whether families want to live in rented quarters in a particular area. If there is a good supply of well-located, inexpensive residential land on which homes can be erected at reasonable prices, there is little inducement for people to spend their money on rent when they can invest it in a house. On the other hand, if residential land near employment centers is scarce and can be fully utilized only by building skyward (as in most of the larger cities), apartment houses become highly desirable. Usually an investment builder need not rely on his own judgment alone. He is guided by the activities of his competitors who are also analyzing the market. Their success or failure may help him determine whether another residential structure is warranted in a given district.

If the indications are that it should be built, the next question is that of style and price range. Should they be high buildings or the two- and three-story structures commonly known as garden apartments? A partial answer is usually provided by the local zoning regulations, which often limit the height of the buildings and the percentage of land that can be built on. But the builder still has to exercise his judgment about what sort of accommodations he can rent most easily and profitably. In many respects, the job of the apartment builder resembles that of the home developer, with the result that many builders have successfully switched from one to the other at will. When the cost of land or the availability of mortgage financing for homes is against constructing houses for the time being, a home builder may spend a year or two developing an apartment house, and then return to the private housing field when it seems more inviting again.

But there are some important differences between the two types of construction that can affect the builder's career. One is that an apartment builder must have the nerves to endure an uncertain market with a heavy inventory on his hands—a headache that a home builder need not face. If a home builder finds a project lagging badly, he only has to discontinue construction, sell the houses already up, and dispose of the remaining land. An apartment builder, on the other hand, has no merchandise until his structure is complete, at which point he is saddled with as many as a hundred or more units that he must rent. There is no such thing as discontinuing business when there is a soft market. Consequently, the young man who plans a future in this field has to have merchandising ability, which he can best gain by a period of employment with a real-estate office that handles leasing for apartment buildings.

His next problem is that of management. True, an apartment house can be built for immediate resale at a profit, as long as it is well rented. But under our tax laws resale by a corporate builder in less than three years means that he is exposed to a heavy income tax on the profit; thus, he can reduce his taxes by holding on to the building for three years, after which his profit is a long-term capital gain, taxable to a maximum of 25 per cent. This means that for at least three years he must operate the property—a task for which he can prepare himself during an apprenticeship in the management division of a real-estate office. This training will be even more important if the investment builder does not sell his structures but prefers to operate them on a long-range basis. This is a problem the home builder does not encounter because the houses he has built and sold soon become only memories.

And while the home builder must be a good coördinator, the apartment builder must be even more proficient in the art of integrating the various trades. For example, if the roofers are late in arriving on the scene of a home development, the builder can easily continue with other phases of the job, leaving the units that are ready for roofing stand idle until the roofers appear. Not so with apartment houses. When a given step of the building process has been accomplished there, nothing moves until the proper trade shows up to continue the work in its proper sequence. Moreover, while a home builder can always sell those houses that are finished, even though others are behind schedule, an apartment builder has no merchandise, and therefore no source of income, until the entire structure is ready for occupancy. From this it is obvious that this field requires considerable coördinating skill, which the novice can get by taking a position, regardless of salary, with a successful apartment builder.

Once we enter the realm of non-residential speculative building, the picture changes radically. This is probably the ultimate refinement in a real-estate career, for it involves virtually every aspect of the industry. Let us, therefore, examine it thoroughly to demonstrate the interplay of the various skills that a man should bring to this field. For the purpose of the discussion, let us assume that he is in business for himself and leave the subsidiary jobs aside for the moment.

A speculative building venture—an office building, a shopping center, an industrial park, a hotel or motel —begins with a survey of the area in which the proposed project is contemplated. This means that the builder must be convinced that there is a need for office space, stores, plant facilities, or guest accommodations from which the property can derive income. Because the tenants of a competitive building where space is already rented out come from various industries and professions, the realty man must know the problems and peculiarities of each so that the space he creates will be suitable to those he is most likely to attract. To do this properly he must be well informed about economic trends and the prevalent practices of various industries and professions. What types of buildings do insurance companies favor for their branch offices? Is it possible to accommodate an automobile showroom in a shopping center? Will the traveling motorist spend the night in a motel forty miles from the nearest city? These are just a few of the typical questions the realty man must ask himself before he knows whether he has a project at all. This is one reason why a solid educational background in economics and commerce is important equipment for the man who wants to succeed in this field.

When he has confirmed his hunch that a building of a given type can succeed in a given location, the speculative builder begins to make discreet inquiries that will lead to his acquiring the necessary land. We say discreet because he cannot commit himself to buy until the economic prospects of the project have been calculated, which naturally cannot be done without some knowledge of the land cost. But once he knows roughly what the land will cost him, he can approach his architect for a sketch of whatever structure can be built on the plot. As an experienced real-estate specialist, he also knows the cost per square or cubic foot to put up such a building. Armed with an estimate, he will next compute the approximate average rental he must charge for the space to make the venture profitable. Whether tenants will pay these rentals is a question he can answer only by falling back on his training and knowledge gained in leasing and in previously placing similar tenants in similar buildings. Finally, he must put out some feelers with lending institutions to find whether mortgage financing for the project will be available in an amount and at an interest rate that will give him the economic leeway he needs. Once he has a good idea of the land costs, construction costs, financing prospects, rentals, and operating expenses, the speculative builder decides whether or not to go through with his plan. Let us assume for the moment that the project has merit and see what comes next.

The first step is to gain control of the necessary land, either through options or outright purchase. This involves some of the most intricate negotiations in the real-estate field. It may be simple, perhaps, to pick up a piece of roadside farm land for a motel, though even here care must be taken not to bid up the price by making the site attractive to a competing motel builder. But the acid test of a real-estate negotiator comes when he tries to assemble a large midtown site for an office building. This involves strategy of a kind that rivals the best efforts of military men. If the land has to be bought from several owners, as is often the case, care must be taken not to allow the price of each succeeding parcel to skyrocket after the first plot has been taken. This is likely to happen as the owners of the site find out why the land is being assembled. To conclude a land assemblage successfully involves camouflage, a knowledge of when to give quarter and when not to budge, and a talent for what airmen call flying by the seat of one's pants.

Shopping around for a suitable mortgage is almost as intricate. Mortgage brokers who represent lending institutions help pave the way, but this does not relieve the investment builder of the final decision. For example, he must know how widely he can "peddle the deal" among lending outfits before he reaches the point of diminishing returns—a feeling he can acquire only through practical experience in the realty investment market. Thoroughly schooled, the builder will know that in many instances it may be bad practice to accept the first offer of a mortgage without having solicited other propositions from other money sources. But he must also know when to stop, lest the loan become shopworn. To reap the richest harvest in the mortgage field calls for an understanding of the workings of the money market, and this comes from a thorough study of economics as well as considerable practical experience in the real-estate and mortgage business.

Next comes the process of negotiating with tenants for the offices, stores, or industrial structures that are being built. The builder spends months getting tenants to sign leases that are to his best advantage. Successful financing is wholly dependent on successful leasing. The builder will probably enjoy the services of a renting agent, but there are exceptions—to wit, the mammoth Socony Mobil Oil Building in New York, for which the owner-builder handled the leasing himself. But regardless of who handles this part, it is the sponsor of the project who must decide whether the rental offered by a prospective tenant is acceptable, whether the tenant's credit rating is good enough for the risk of a long-term commitment, and how the space should be apportioned. The last consideration can be of the utmost importance in a shopping center, for example. Here a retailer might offer a very tempting lease for a store in a location that the builder feels should be reserved for a shop of a different kind. An error of judgment in mislocating such a tenant because of the lure of high rentals can throw the entire shopping center out of balance and threaten its success. Here, again, practical experience in the leasing field is invaluable to the investment builder. And, finally, there is the task of managing the property once it is built and occupied. Suffice it to say that in this regard all of the facets of good management practice come into play.

As we said before, non-residential investment building is the acme of the realty profession. Clearly, it is not an undertaking for a novice but rather one to which the novice can aspire, especially since it also requires considerable capital. But for the man whose objective is investment building, there are definite concrete preparatory steps to take. To begin with, he should get as thorough an education as he can in economics, law, and commerce. In addition, he should train himself to be a keen observer of every imaginable form of commercial and industrial enterprise. It is too late for him to look for the drawbacks of the advertising business when an advertising agency is at his door to negotiate a major lease. And it is too late for him to bone up on governmental procedures if he has to decide whether or not to build a plant for a small perfume maker on the day Congress is debating lower import duties on cosmetic products. Knowledge of the probabilities in such situations must be at his fingertips, or else his risk is immeasurable. This means continuous study of economic journals and writings on tax law, labor, and the like, along with the various published discussions of the realty market. Informal self-education never really ends for the real-estate speculator.

His practical training can begin in a number of ways, but it should eventually include experience in all areas of the industry. Going to work for an investment-building company is one short cut. But unless the young recruit shows an unusual amount of drive and initiative, his efforts along these lines are likely to be lost in the organizational shuffle. This means that such an apprenticeship must eventually lead to a break for independence, a break that could be dangerously premature. This is a field where breadth of experience counts heavily, and there is no better way than to gather it far and wide.

It is therefore preferable to avoid short cuts and to start work in a brokerage office that deals heavily in commercial leasing and sales, in land assemblage, and if possible in mortgages. More than likely, no one agency will offer all of these in satisfactory measure, so you would do well to remain mobile in the early years. Since this is especially true of the mortgage field, it is advisable for a prospective investment builder to tie in with a mortgage specialist or a lending institution. These need not be lean years. With a good educational background and a talent for real-estate dealing, a young man can make some profitable deals even while he amasses experience for his ultimate career. Somewhere along the line, too, he should acquaint himself with property management—a specialty that will undoubtedly be part of his training in a large real-estate office. During these early years, a realty man will probably have sufficient contact with the building trades and with the legal and architectural professions to absorb what he needs to know in order to embark on his own first venture.

What, then, are the rewards of a career in investment

building? We must confess that there is no yardstick to guide us beyond the knowledge that huge fortunes have been made and lost in this field. Yes, men have been wiped out by errors of judgment or by unexpected reverses in the general economy. But we must assume, first, that anyone who is ready to tackle a major building project has already accumulated substantial funds as evidence of his capacity and judgment. It is not likely that a man will be ready mentally and emotionally but not financially for a major building venture or vice versa. The three usually go together. In any event, if a career in investment building is planned and executed with patience, logic, initiative, and a well-developed sense of values and timing, it can lead to economic heights that dwarf the workaday concepts of earnings, percentage yields, or security.

CHAPTER VI

Realty Finance

Fortunately for modern society, few have taken to heart the advice that Shakespeare's character Polonius gave his son: "Neither a borrower nor a lender be." Today, without lending and borrowing, the average American family could not own a home, and the multitude of buildings in which we work, shop, and seek amusements would probably not exist. Anyone who has ever shopped for a home knows that the cost of a building or a piece of land is usally beyond the average person's purse. Few prospective home buyers have accumulated the $15,000 or more it costs to buy a house. Nor do even the most successful realty operators have the millions in ready cash necessary to buy a major piece of property outright.

Obviously what is needed is a loan facility that will supply enough money to make up the difference between the price of a property and the amount of cash the purchaser can spare. And such loan facilities exist—in the form of institutions that hold people's money in trust for one purpose or another. Let us look first at a bank or a savings-and-loan association. Both are institutions where ordinary people keep their savings for protection against fire and theft and for the income they bring in when invested. For the bank or savings-and-loan association to pay this income—say, 3 per-cent interest —it must in turn lend these funds to someone else for enough more than 3 per cent to cover its costs of operations and still bring a profit after the depositor is paid his interest. Similarly, a life-insurance company is custodian of the premiums paid into it by the people whose lives it insures. But these premiums must also be invested for income; how else could the company pay out $10,000 on the death of a person who paid only $6,000 in premiums while he was alive? But let us not forget that these institutions have only temporary control over the money of their depositors or policy holders. These companies cannot afford to invest foolishly because at any time they must have enough funds ready for a depositor who wants to make a large withdrawal or for paying a policy holder's insurance claim. Clearly, an institution like this has to put its funds in investments that offer a high degree of security. And loans on real property, if made wisely, provide this outlet.

Here are some of the reasons why: A mortgage loan is a loan that has for security a pledge in the form of a bond given by the borrower. The pledge says that if the borrower is unable to repay the loan with interest as he agreed, the lender can take over the property itself. To make sure that a mortgage loan is secure, it is ordinarily made for less than the full value of the property —anywhere from 50 to 65 per cent in most cases, although government-backed mortgages have a higher ratio. Therefore, if the property is properly appraised before the loan is made, the property, which is the ultimate collateral, is worth more than the amount put up against it. Consequently, in an emergency the loan can usually be recovered by selling the property.

Here we have one of the main differences between mortgages for private homes and those for income-producing properties. When a person seeks a mortgage loan for a house, the lender has to base his calculations in part on the borrower's income and his reliability in such matters as paying bills and keeping his job. Thus, it is a question of a personal credit rating, since the real estate—in this case, the home—does not produce income. However, when a mortgage is being considered for an income-producing property, the owner's personal-credit standing is a secondary matter; this is especially true if the real estate is to be owned by a corporation. What the mortgage lender wants to know in this instance is whether the property, with efficient management, will earn sufficient income to meet the debt obligations, operating expenses, real-estate taxes, and a margin of safety. The lender also wants to know that those in charge of managing the property are capable of making it produce its potential income, or that the owner-user of the property, such as the manufacturer who occupies his own factory, is engaged in a soundly conceived and operated business. Given such assurances, a lending institution has no qualms about investing the funds in its trust in a real-estate mortgage.

This is a very rough description of mortgage lending, but it should serve as a point of departure for examining some of the many careers in this field. And we might add that this is one area of the real-estate industry where the salaried employee plays as large a role as the independent businessman or commission broker.

Perhaps the simplest form of mortgage financing is that used in the purchase of a home. Asssuming that buyer and seller have agreed on a price, either one of them or the broker who brought them together must go to a lending institution—say, a bank—to discuss financing with the mortgage officer. He is a man who has obtained his training in one of several ways. He may have started in the banking business and specialized in the mortgage department. He may have had some background as a mortgage broker, possibly as an employee of a mortgage company (a concern that will be discussed later). Or he may have been in the real-estate business and made appraising his specialty.

As mortgage officer, he knows that the man who wants to buy the house needs some sort of suitable financing. But he cannot be given too large a loan because the bank's mortgage committee or board of directors is not likely to approve a mortgage that is out of proportion to the value of the house or the income of the applicant. And the mortgage officer also knows that he would not be doing the prospective home owner a favor by saddling him with a loan he cannot afford to carry, even though he is willing to try. The mortgage officer has to have the experience and training to know enough about economics in general to judge whether a family with a given income and given financial obligations can afford to carry a particular mortgage. If the answer is no, the mortgage officer has to handle the applicant much like a family physician who must sometimes advise a patient to eat less of a favorite food for the sake of his health. If, however, the mortgage officer feels the loan is justifiable, he must be prepared to stick to his guns when the issue arises before the mortgage committee or the board of directors. This means that he must be a man whose educational background, judgment, and convictions impress the directors enough so that they feel safe in relying on him.

A good mortgage officer must never cease to keep abreast of changes in such factors as the cost of living, taxes, and the prospects of various occupations. For example, he must be aware that just because it was once safe to grant a mortgage equal to twice a man's annual income, this is no longer the case because of rising living costs. And he must be sufficiently schooled in occupational analysis to know that a junior executive in a growing industry can handle a slightly larger mortgage than a man with an equal income whose trade offers little opportunity for increased income. If a mortgage officer has a good performance record—the num‹ ber of loans repaid on schedule compared to those that brought trouble—his job can eventually lead to a higher rank. Depending on his experience, the size of the institution, and the scope of his jurisdiction (whether he handles only home loans or all of the mortgage business), his salary will vary from $7,500 to $20,000 a year. It will be substantially larger, however, if he succeeds in increasing business by placing mortgages on highly attractive properties during periods when the supply of lendable funds exceeds the demand. This requires a salesman who can handle very sensitive merchandise— other people's money.

Assuming that the bank's mortgage officer has tentatively approved a loan, the next man to come into the picture is the appraiser. The bank needs his services to make certain that the loan it grants is sufficiently less than the market value of the house. If its policy, for example, is to lend only 60 per cent of the market value, the appraiser must find that the house is truly worth $20,000 before a mortgage of $12,000 will be made. Because appraising is an important part of real estate and reaches far beyond the task of figuring out the value of a home, let us examine it in detail now.

As the term itself implies, an appraiser is able to determine by virtue of his specialized knowledge what a piece of real estate is worth. And while realty men will tell you that three different appraisers may find three different values for the same piece of property, the fact remains that a professional appraisal carries tremendous authority not only within the industry but also in the courts and other governmental agencies. Here, indeed, is a vast field with many career opportunities for both salaried employees and independent agents.

The situation of the home purchase described above is one possibility. In this instance, an appraiser must look at the house, the land, and the neighborhood and then determine with accuracy whether its market value is sufficiently high to support the mortgage that is sought. In other words, will the loan that the purchaser has applied for be no more than the lender's standard percentage of the total value? And will the value of the house stand up through the years as the amount of the loan reduces gradually through amortization? It is this valuation of the property that the mortgage officer must rely on when he presents the loan application to the committee or the board of directors.

But this is only a small part of an appraiser's work. When lending institutions are asked to place mortgages on major properties such as office buildings, apartment houses, shopping centers, hotels, motels, and industrial plants, they also use the services of an appraiser—often a large firm in the appraising business. Their objective, too, is to find out whether the loan under consideration is warranted by the property's market value. Appraisers are also retained by prospective buyers or sellers of real estate. A realty man who is considering the purchase of a particular parcel has to find out whether the price asked by the seller or the amount he is offering is closest to the property's market value. By the same token, the seller wants to know how much he can realistically ask for a given property.

To establish the value of a single private home is a relatively simple procedure for an appraiser, although many factors enter into it. He can readily establish the value of the land by checking on the price of similar plots in the same or a comparable neighborhood. He can also figure out the home's replacement cost, using his training for this career. From the replacement cost he must deduct something for the age of the house. Perhaps it has become somewhat old-fashioned in the years since it was built, or it may have undergone some unusual wear and tear. Finally, after taking into account any other unusual circumstances—a rare architectural style, an extraordinary scenic view, a plot that is particularly large or small for the size of the house—he has found the value of the property.

When he deals with income-producing properties, however, the task is not so simple. He must go through all of the above steps, too, but then he has considerably more to do. For example, he has to determine whether the income the property produces is in line with the value he has established by using the other yardsticks. This is what is called capitalizing the return. It means this: Assuming that he is appraising an apartment house of a type that he knows should earn 8 per cent of its market value each year, he must find out whether this income is being produced. If he learns, for instance, that the building brings in $8,000 a year, he knows that a $100,000 valuation is about right. He can then check this against the valuation he figured out earlier. In the matter of depreciation, he must also be more particular. If his examination of the building shows that the heating plant will have to be replaced within three years, he either has to know or find out the cost, which is then amortized over the proper number of years and deducted from the building's net income. This, too, affects the final valuation of the property.

If the appraiser is dealing with a store or hotel property, he has to take all of the above steps plus still others. He must analyze the market for buildings of this kind to see whether they now have their former income potential. For example, there may be nothing wrong structurally with a certain New England textile mill or the land it stands on—nothing except that the textile industry has moved to the South, and there is little else for which the building can be used. Or the construction of a shopping center near an existing one may affect the value of the latter, for better or for worse. If competition in the area is favorable to increasing business for everybody, then it increases the value of all the store buildings. However, if the neighborhood is already overloaded with retail shops, all the stores tend to go down in value. These are all considerations that play a constant part in the appraiser's work.

Condemnations make up another field in which the services of an appraiser are vital. When the federal, a state, or a municipal government wants a particular piece of property for a public improvement—a highway, a new courthouse, or the like—it can exercise what is known as the right of eminent domain. This right, which has its historical origin in the royal prerogatives of feudal times, entitles the government to take possession of property it needs for the public good without first obtaining the consent of the owner. However, in our democratic system the law provides that the government agency that takes the property must compensate the owner through what is known as a condemnation award. The amount of the award should be equal to the property's market value, a figure that obviously is debatable when one considers the possibly conflicting interests of the government and the property owner.

Before the government begins any condemnation proceedings, therefore, it hires an appraiser to estimate how much it will have to pay in a condemnation award. If the public improvement justifies the cost of condemnation, the government will go ahead with its plan and acquire the necessary real estate, offering the owners the contemplated award. Sometimes an owner decides that the proffered award is insufficient compensation and plans to appeal it to the courts. Before he can do this, he should be able to prove that his property is really worth more than the government's offer. Thus, the owner must also hire an appraiser. If his appraiser comes up with a value higher than the government award, the owner can take his case to court, where the respective appraisers testify as opposing experts. On the basis of this testimony, the court eventually decides what would be a fair award.

Appraisers are often called on to render expert testimony in court proceedings other than those involving condemnations. For example, say that a group of partners bought an office building some years ago. Now a dispute arises and one of them wants to buy out the others and get full control of the property. But the price he offers is unsatisfactory to them because they feel that the building has increased in value in a rising realty market. One appraisal of the property might solve their problem; or, if they still cannot agree, appraisals made by each side may end up in a compromise. A situation similar to this that finally ended up in court led to the historic auction of the seventy-story building at 40 Wall Street, in New York City, when the court set a minimum price of $17,000,000. Another frequent use of appraisers is involved with leaseholds. Long-term ground leases usually provide that future rentals will be set at a fixed rate of the future appraised value. The method of selecting the appraisers is specified in the lease.

The appraising profession is one of the most respected activities in real estate; in fact, it is a highly regarded specialty in all fields. And appraisers, like their brethren in other lines, maintain a thoroughly professional attitude toward their work and their contacts in the business world. Their associations—such as the American Institute of Real Estate Appraisers and the Society of Residential Appraisers—encourage a professional atmosphere and guard their membership standards zealously. Many appraisers are also active in other phases of the industry, though most are proudest of the field in which they have gained professional status. In theory at least, any real-estate man can do appraisal work since his estimate of a property's value has meaning only to the person who asked for it. But a realty broker who also does appraising as a side line is not an appraiser in terms of a chosen career. For those who pick it as a career, it can provide both highly satisfying work and, under the right circumstances, an attractive income.

Since property appraisal calls into play just about every aspect of the economy, an appraiser has to be a man of wide knowledge. How else is he to determine the proper value of a warehouse in an office-building neighborhood, or that of a motel on the fringe of a busy airport whose landing strip is not large enough to accommodate jet planes? Such factors have a great deal to do with market values, and it is the appraiser's job to analyze them with reasonable accuracy. Clearly, this calls for an understanding of matters other than property lines and brick and mortar.

Above all, an appraiser's primary training should be in the real-estate field. (It must be assumed, of course, that he also has a background in general academic studies.) To prepare himself for his career, he should start out as a salesman in an active brokerage office. There is no better way to develop a keen sense of realty values than to deal with people who are buying and selling land and buildings. The market place is traditionally a good place to learn the business facts of life. Meanwhile, the future appraiser can make a reasonably comfortable living while he prepares himself for the broker's examination and his ultimate professional specialty. Another stopping place on the road to appraisership should be a lending institution of some kind. Here, the future specialist will get a somewhat different look at real property. Until now he has seen it through the eyes of the seller and the buyer. Now he will see property through the eyes of the mortgage lender. This is important because it is a less biased view. The mortgage lender is not trying to inflate or depress the value of a parcel. All he wants to know is its market value so that the loan he makes will be protected by the intrinsic worth of the collateral.

Seeing at first hand how this value is determined by experts in the day-to-day process of mortgage lending is invaluable training for a future appraiser. At the same time, too, he would be wise to take advantage of any courses in appraising that are offered in his community. In some cases, such classes are given as part of postgraduate or extension courses of universities. In others, intensive courses in appraising are available in specialized business schools. Either type is acceptable, but we strongly recommend some formal training for this field.

Once an appraiser has attained full professional status, he may find it economically more attractive to go to work for someone else or at least to supplement his specialty with a general realty practice. If he is happy in a thriving real-estate office, we suggest that he stay there until his appraising activities no longer allow time for run-of-the-mill realty work. There is a practical reason for this. If an appraiser is affiliated with an active real-estate agency whose owners know about his specialty, any appraisals that are requested of the agency will become his task, thus bringing him fees in addition to the income he earns as a salesman or broker. If his work as an appraiser brings in enough business and prestige, he may in time become a partner. On the other hand, if his reputation as a specialist makes his association with a realty outfit unnecessary, he may decide to break these business ties and open an office of his own.

To understand the economics behind this decision, let us take a look at the fees that are generally paid for appraisals. Though these vary with each area of the country, in most localities they are tied to the overall size of the property rather than its price. This is the case because if a fee were directly related to the property value, the motives of the appraiser would always be open to question. Consequently, a fee is based on the amount of work an appraisal involves. For an ordinary one-family house in the New York metropolitan area, for example, an appraiser charges from $50 to $100. For appraising a thirty-story skyscraper, on the other hand, he can earn as much as $10,000. It is easy to see why an active appraiser, especially one engaged in handling large properties, would eventually become reluctant to share his fee with a real-estate firm merely for the sake of having this formal connection.

However, none but the top appraisers in the field constantly appraise skyscrapers and shopping centers. There simply are not that many of them. So it becomes a matter of deciding whether an appraisal practice will support an office. At one extreme, we have an appraiser in a rural area, where appraising is never more than part of a realty business. At the other, we have an eminent specialist in a large city, where assignments are so complex that he employs a staff of appraisers and other personnel to lay the groundwork for the overall valuation, which he ultimately makes himself. By and large, an independent appraiser does not depend heavily on the social part of business life for success. Here, then, is a field for the candidate who prefers not being an organization man.

However, there are interesting career opportunities for appraisers who prefer salaried employment in large institutions. Needless to say, any lending institution that transacts real-estate loans on a daily basis is likely to employ its own appraisal staff. For one thing, it is more economical, since the appraiser's salary is usually less than the fees of outside appraisers. But another reason, which outweighs the cost factor, is that each lending institution has its own procedure and forms, and prefers to work with appraisers who are familiar with these requirements.

For instance, a particular life-insurance company will feel that the value of property is more dependent on neighborhood, transportation facilities, and the like than on its physical condition. In other words, the company's top men feel that while it is always possible to improve property structurally, there is little that can be done about its location. However, the officers of another insurance company or bank will not agree with this theory. They feel, instead, that the value of a piece of land reflects the location automatically and, therefore, that the more important consideration is the structural soundness and the usefulness of the improvements on that land. Differences like this are often so subtle that only experts understand them. But they are sufficient cause why large, active lending institutions prefer to hire their own appraisers or at least use the same outside appraisers regularly.

The federal government also offers positions for appraisers. These jobs, for the most part, are in the local offices of the Federal Housing Administration, where applications for mortgages insured by the F.H.A. are handled. While the F.H.A. does not make direct loans on property, it does insure some loans made by private institutions and must, therefore, be equally sure that the value of the collateral is sound. This government agency has a wide field of activity, insuring loans not only on private homes but on rental and coöperative apartments as well. To some extent, the Veterans Administration is in the same business, since it guarantees mortgages on houses bought by former servicemen. The V.A.'s loan-guaranty division also has an appraising staff. Any of these agencies, concerned as they are with property acquisition and development, have to determine the market value of land, existing buildings, and future construction. Positions within these government agencies are under civil-service jurisdiction and command salaries ranging from $6,000 to $13,000, depending on seniority and experience, under the schedule of civil-service ratings. Applications for this type of position should be made on a standard government form. This will get the job-seeker a chance to compete in a civil-service examination, which will show if he is qualified for the job.

On the state or municipal level, there is also a civil-service job for the appraiser—that of the tax assessor. To understand the functions of this position, let us look for a moment at the method by which most American communities collect the revenues needed to administer their local services. It is traditional that the costs of operating a municipality are borne by residents and businessmen who own property in the town. At one time, this meant nearly everybody, because rental accommodations for home, office, or shop were virtually nonexistent. This was the most widespread and equitable form of taxation known to our ancestors. It was presumed then, and it is still true to some extent now, that by taxing property owners according to the size and value of their land and buildings, a municipality would make them pay for local services in direct proportion to the amount of these services they consumed. This concept has been somewhat distorted by our economy becoming more complex through the years. Some of the local residents who are most able to contribute to municipal revenue live in rented quarters and therefore contribute to the local tax only indirectly as part of the rent they pay. The landlord who actually makes the tax payments may live elsewhere and not partake of the municipal services at all. In a sense, it is the property and not its owner that is being taxed nowadays. In support of this is the theory that it is the property that is getting the benefit of municipal services, such as fire and police protection, regardless of who may occupy it.

The main problem of administering real-estate tax is that of levying it fairly. If Mr. Jones lives in a six-room house on a half-acre plot and his neighbor, Mr. Smith, lives in a twelve-room house on a one-acre site, it seems only fair that Smith should pay twice as much taxes as Jones. And in most communities he would. To keep the tax ratio equitable, municipalities need an appraiser who is known as the assessor. Not all comparisons are as simple as the illustration above. Perhaps Smith's house and plot are exactly twice the size of Jones's, but Jones's property may be in a better part of town and therefore may be worth more than Smith's. Or even if the houses stand side by side, Smith's, though larger, may also be considerably older and show it. Therefore, his may' not be worth exactly twice as much as Jones's. To establish the proper relationship between all the properties in town takes an appraiser. This is why assessors should, and usually do, come from the ranks of appraisers.

There is a marked difference, however, between the work of an appraiser and that of an assessor. In fact, their procedures are almost exactly reversed. An appraiser tries to establish an absolute value for a property by comparing it with similar properties. An assessor tries to establish comparative values based on the absolute values of properties. Let us illustrate what we mean. An appraiser may be retained by a buyer, seller, or lender to find out what a given house and plot are worth on the market. He does this by finding out what comparable parcels have brought or might bring in a free-market sale. He adjusts for differences in age, location, and design when he compares the property in question with other parcels. The result should be a fair market price for the house and its plot. The assessor, on the other hand, takes the market values of individual properties, as far as they are known or can be established, and determines what relationship they have to each other.

Regardless of how the comparative values are determined, appraising principals are involved. It stands to reason, therefore, that the local assessor should be an appraiser by profession, or at least a real-estate man with substantial appraising experience. This, however, is not universally true. In many municipalities, especially smaller ones, the assessor's job is a political office, either by election or appointment. It is very fortunate that many local political organizations make certain that appointees or candidates for the assessor's office are qualified professionally for the work. In some cases, however, qualifications play a lesser role than the candidate's connections in political circles.

In the smaller municipalities, there is not enough assessing to require a full-time employee. In cities with populations of at least 200,000, on the other hand, it is an entirely different matter. While the chief assessor (often also known as the tax commissioner) may not be a professional appraiser, he does not personally go out and assess properties. This task is assigned to a group of assessors who are qualified appraisers. Theirs are civil-service jobs with salaries that seldom exceed $8,500 a year. As a rule, municipalities do not actively revaluate every property in town every year. Generally, assessments are made for newly built improvements, including new structures and additions to existing ones.

If property is involved in a sale and the price paid indicates that the assessment is considerably out of line with the newly established value, the assessor must go back and reassess, in order to keep comparative values in proper ratio. Indications are that more and more cities are waking up to the fact that more conscientious and accurate assessing is of immeasurable value to good administration. This means that young men with experience as appraisers can look forward to civil-service careers in this field.

But because the average community does let its assessments for the tax rolls slip out of kilter in the course of many years, certain inequities tend to arise that have to be corrected from time to time. For example, while houses assessed a decade ago were properly evaluated, real-estate costs have risen since that time. Meanwhile, newly built structures have been evaluated on the basis of current prices. This, of course, creates an inequity until older properties are also reassessed. The result in many communities is that the situation can be remedied only by a complete revaluation of all the real estate within their boundaries. This is a mammoth task, and the municipality usually retains a firm of professionals to handle it.

Concerns of this type are so in demand that towns wishing to have their real estate reassessed must notify them more than a year in advance to reserve their services. While such valuation concerns provide jobs for all types of personnel, including map makers and the like, the most important phase of their work calls for the services of appraisers. We are inclined to think that this part of the profession will grow in future years to a point where it will provide a steady flow of employment opportunities with salaries ranging from $10,000 to $20,000 a year, depending on experience and length of service.

Turning back to the financing field itself, we come to a rather new type of operation—the mortgage company. An outgrowth of large development housing, mortgage companies have become instrumental in arranging the home-loan packages that expedite the financing needed for selling large groups of houses. As was explained earlier, a home buyer wishing to obtain a mortgage must shop around for a loan, perhaps with the aid of the seller or broker, among the various lending institutions that finance home purchases. Each property is normally considered on an individual basis, with the lender appraising it to determine what the amount and terms of the loan should be. The sale usually depends on the ability of one of the principals to arrange a suitable mortgage. How much more complex, then, is it to sell a hundred houses in a development, let alone several thousand, with suitable financing. It would be infinitely more complex were it not for the post-war growth of mortgage companies whose main function is to arrange for loans to finance sales at developments.

Mortgage companies are able to package the necessary financing because of the characteristics of tract housing. In a typical subdivision, one or more basic model houses are offered for reproduction on a large number of sites. Within a relatively narrow range of variation, all of the homes in the subdivision are of about equal value. If, for example, a developer is showing three basic models, there are only three houses to appraise, regardless of the fact that several hundred of them are to be built. Land values tend to be about the same throughout the subdivision, too. If, therefore, the typical plot is 100 by 100 feet, it is fairly easy to appraise each site; the only problems are that some sites are slightly larger than others, and that some have more favorable locations by virtue of the view or terrain. Because a portfolio of a hundred or more mortgages can easily be assembled by appraising only a handful of prototypes, it is possible for one lending institution to take care of a development mortgage package running to millions of dollars.

Such packages are usually assembled by a special mortgage broker who provides the liaison between builder and lender. It is his function to advise the builder on the most advantageous way to lay out his community and on the most salable design of the houses themselves. When the builder has evolved a satisfactory plan, the mortgage company gives him the green light on the project, while it seeks the necessary financial backing from one of the lending institutions with which it does business. The mortgage company may also arrange the temporary financing—the construction loan—needed by the builder to get his project under way.

The art of operating a successful mortgage company involves knowing not only which institution has funds available for a development of a given size but also which institutions are interested in financing houses of a particular type and price range in a particular area. For example, there are lenders in San Francisco who are always ready to finance a tract on the peninsula but are not fond of mortgages in Marin County, or vice versa. Some lending institutions favor houses of traditional design but hesitate to finance contemporary homes. Sometimes a mortgage company has to go quite far afield, possibly to another section of the country, to place a block of loans on favorable terms. At other times —especially when lendable funds are in short supply— a mortgage company may even have to warehouse loans. This means making loans to home purchasers out of its own funds until the mortgages can be placed with an institution. Lending institutions like working with mortgage companies because it reduces their administrative chores. By examining only the subdivision tract and the model houses, a lending institution lays the groundwork for a sizable portfolio of mortgages, which will be delivered as a package. In many cases, even the servicing of these loans, once they are delivered, remains the task of the mortgage concern. This includes investigating borrowers' credit before loans are made and taking care of monthly billing and accounting as soon as the home owners start to make their regular payments.

If the postwar trend of tract housing continues—and indications are that it will—attractive careers will continue to be available in the mortgage-company field. The talent needed for success in this work is a blend of judgment, salesmanship, and administrative efficiency. The whole trick of this business consists of being able to recognize a salable housing development before it is started, to sell the builder on using your mortgage company as his agent, to sell the loan package to a lending institution on favorable terms, and to administer the month-to-month servicing of the loans as economically as possible.

For a particularly successful future in this career, a young man should have some experience in home selling or building as well as in financing. It is also essential that he be able to read blueprints of land subdivisions and home designs with an eye to determining the sales potential and the general feasibility of a builder's plans. Builders—by nature an optimistic group—sometimes fail to recognize the pitfalls of their proposed projects. But before a mortgage man can promise a developer a financing package, he must convince himself that the houses to be erected will be in a desirable location and are so designed as to be easily sold at the projected price. At the same time, the mortgage-company executive must know enough about construction to determine roughly whether the builder is planning his colony on a sound financial footing. After sales have been made and construction has been started, there is little he can do but pick up the pieces if the developer finds out that he will lose money on each house because of unforeseen structural or engineering problems or unknown obstacles in the terrain.

A man with a background in construction—either as an engineer or as a field man with a home builder—has an advantage in a career in a mortgage company. Experience in residential real-estate brokerage is also helpful. For one thing, it gives a man a working knowledge of the market—of the housing needs of families in various income groups, of features that make houses easy or difficult to sell, and of the financing problems that arise with every home sale. For another, it trains a man in the art of salesmanship, a skill that he must develop for a career in a mortgage company.

It is possible also to approach such a career from the financing end—that is, from a previous job with a lending institution. With a proper grounding in the techniques of assembling a mortgage portfolio, especially packages of home loans, a young man can readily turn to a more profitable occupation in the mortgage-company field. Having assembled loans for a lender, he is well equipped to sell such loans to other lenders. He knows their preferences and reactions, and his judgment should then be keen enough to obtain the best possible terms in the sale of mortgages to lending institutions.

It is difficult to assess the standard financial yield in this occupation. Mortgage companies are essentially small ventures with relatively little capital, though they transact a sizable dollar volume of business. The only capital they require is for direct office overhead, and for temporary financing when it is advantageous to warehouse loans in anticipation of a more favorable market.

However, there is no minimum capital requirement because a mortgage company can be successful, without
warehousing activity, by relying entirely on its turnover
and servicing of loans. Nor does this operation require
large staffs—not in the upper echelons, at least. It takes
only two or three go-getters to assemble a list of builder-
clients and to negotiate with lenders for mortgage com-
mitments. After all, how many large housing developments are started in any locale? By and large, a mortgage company's income depends on its executives' ability to create business and on the company's location in
terms of new housing construction.

In the lower echelons there are only a few positions
with high incomes. For one, if the man in charge of servicing loans is efficient in management matters, he can
make an enviable niche for himself. Most mortgage investors are prepared to pay about one-half of 1 per cent
of the mortgage principal for servicing. In the case of a
$15,000 home loan, this means an annual fee of $75
for making monthly collections and keeping records of
interest, amortization, and escrow funds. In a portfolio
of mortgages averaging $15,000 on a subdivision of a
hundred houses, this means a fee of $7,500 paid by the
lender. The less the mortgage company needs of this
$7,500 to maintain the accounts properly, the more val-
uable is the man in charge of servicing, and his salary
and bonuses will reflect this. (In all fairness, we should
add that many lending institutions do their own servicing to retain this fee for themselves. Some even service
loans for secondary lenders—that is, investors to whom
they have resold mortgages they made.) Large mortgage companies also hire their own appraisers and engineers, but most depend on independent practitioners.
Similarly, most mortgage companies also retain independent credit investigators to check on home-loan applicants before mortgages are granted. It is clear from

this that only the top echelons—the people who actually negotiate the loan with builder and lending institution —are truly in the real-estate industry.

The same is true of the mortgage broker who flourishes primarily in the large cities. He arranges mortgages for heavy construction—office buildings, apartment houses, shopping centers, industrial parks, hotels, etc. His task is somewhat more complex, because he has to appraise the sales potential of a commodity that is less predictable than a model house. As we mentioned in an earlier chapter, the risk of home building is more controllable than that of heavy construction. If a developer has trouble selling the first ten houses, he can sell the remainder of his land and discontinue the project. Not so with an office building or a hotel. No prophet can forecast the patronage a new hotel will get. And while an office building is seldom started without some indication that certain major companies will rent sizable space in it, its success or failure cannot be determined until after construction is completed and operating expenses have been tested in actual practice.

Consequently, the task of the mortgage broker who deals in large construction—as well as in large mortgages for existing buildings—requires an intimate knowledge of the real-estate market in its most fickle form. For this reason, brokers in this kind of financing have relatively small staffs. For a man to find his way into the top ranks of such a company, he must have thorough schooling in all phases of the realty market, including sales-and-leasing brokerage, construction, appraising, and a smattering of architecture and engineering. There are also some mortgage brokers in this part of the industry who employ their own engineering and architectural staffs, but they do not constitute the majority. It would be unrealisic to ignore the fact that this is a field in which a man with good social ties to the sources of large mortgage funds enjoys a definite advantage over his colleagues.

Brokers who deal in second, or junior, mortgages move in a world of their own. Since this is a somewhat more risky business, it is also more lucrative. Firms that deal in secondary financing are not as elaborately staffed as their first-mortgage counterparts, nor do they enter a venture at as early a stage. The mortgages they handle are normally placed among private investors and are traded almost like securities. A $100,000 second mortgage may be negotiable for no more than $30,000 when it is first made, but its market value increases as it approaches its maturity date—provided, of course, that the property it covers remains in a sound financial condition. If anything threatens the health of a property—neighborhood deterioration, unduly heavy vacancies, and the like—the value of the mortgage on it declines until some favorable turn of events, such as a sale, sends it upward again. More than any other operation in real estate, the second-mortgage market is one that none but the most widely experienced realty man should enter—and even then only after his other dealings have led him into it. It requires know-how, salted with courage and peppered with shrewdness.

The same is true of equity financing, which is a relatively new activity in the real-estate world. In its most common form, equity financing involves group investment through syndication. This means that a costly property is up for sale for a greater amount of cash down than any one investor can conveniently muster; to solve the problem, a real-estate syndicator or syndicate manager assembles a group of investors who jointly buy the property for the return it is calculated to yield. Through a variety of formulas, the syndicate manager receives a return higher than the normal yield on whatever investment he makes, if any. This additional return compensates him for the work of finding and analyzing the property, putting up his own money as a deposit, assembling the investors into a group, and administering the affairs of the syndicate during its existence. This form of financing has accounted for some of the largest real-estate deals made during the past decade and can be expected to continue as a potent force in the realty market.

Careers in equity financing, like those in second mortgages, are not embarked on in the same way a man opens a store and invites business. Rather, they are outgrowths of other activities in the real-estate field, notably personal investing. When an investor finds a property he would like to buy but which is beyond his own means to acquire, he usually invites like-minded investors to come along with him. If his deals are large enough, he may find himself syndicating so many properties among so many investors that this has become his primary business. Very large syndicate concerns provide some employment for salesmen who sell pieces of the property to the general public. But, beyond this, equity financing is a personal venture for which there is no real career pattern. Again, it is a field with large returns, particularly for those who have capital of their own to invest or ready access to other investors.

From this glance at real-estate financing and its allied activities, it can be readily seen that there are many possible careers—both for men who want to work for themselves and those who prefer salaried employment. Because most realty transactions depend so heavily on outside financing, this kind of operation can be one of the most rewarding in the industry.

CHAPTER VII

Some Related Fields

On the fringe of the real-estate business are a number of careers that are sometimes considered realty occupations and therefore bear brief examination here. For the most part, they involve not dealing with real property but rather with the people who deal with it. Because of the vastness and complexity of the realty field, there are many ways in which people can serve the industry without being directly in it.

Writing About Real Estate

One fringe career that is not a part of the real-estate business but requires a thorough knowledge of it is writing about real estate. There are many ways in which a writing career and real estate can be combined. The most obvious of these is as a newspaper writer on realty subjects. While most of the members of the National Association of Real Estate Editors started as ordinary newspapermen covering news beats of all sorts, today they are expert analysts of the realty field. It is a safe bet that, to a man, they could succeed quite handsomely in the realty business. But, instead, they have chosen to stick to their typewriters, acting as a sort of liaison between the real-estate world and the man in the street.

Generally, a real-estate editor or writer for a daily newspaper plans a career in journalism. His income, therefore, is in line with that of most newspaper men, varying with the prevailing pay scales of each locality

and his own experience and position. Some of these specialists have eventually turned to media other than daily
newspapers. One of them, for example, has achieved
considerable prestige as a writer for the magazine *Architectural Forum* after resigning his post as real-estate
editor of one of New York's leading daily papers. Others
have joined or started trade journals in the realty field.
It is difficult to assess the income potential of such pub-
lications, largely because it is so closely tied to the volume of advertising they carry and the space rates they
charge. But there is no doubt that many a journalist
has made a more than comfortable living as the owner,
editor, or employee of a trade publication. We might
add that some of these journals and magazines do not
cover the entire real-estate field but only some specialized area of it, such as appraising, prefabricated-house
manufacture, plumbing fixtures, and the like.

Another writing career with a real-estate interest lies
in the promotional field. In larger communities nowadays, realty concerns that hope to improve their business volume by placing their names before the public
pay substantial sums for the services of a public-relations counselor. In some instances, these services are
little more than press agentry—placing publicity in the
various media to entice the public to conduct business
with the concern involved. This in itself calls for a public-relations man with considerable writing skill and
good contacts among the editors who have the final say
on whether a particular publicity item will get into print.

Lately, this simple form of press agentry has been
giving way to the more sober, more delicate art of public
relations. No longer does a real-estate man tell his public-relations counselor, "I don't care what they print
about me so long as they spell my name right." Today's
knowledgeable realty man wants his public-relations
aide to formulate a long-range policy that helps create

what Madison Avenue has come to call a corporate image. It is not merely a matter of placing a client's name before the public in any old way but one of presenting him in such a way that he will gain an enviable business reputation.

Public-relations specialists deal with realty men at all levels nowadays, especially in the large cities. Some P-R men, as they are called, run their own agencies either by themselves or with a few employees, most of whom are writers. Others are account executives in large public-relations firms. Still others are employed directly by the real-estate concern they serve exclusively. Since public relations is an occupation in its own right and not directly a part of this discussion, let us only explain that it can be a highly satisfying career. Naturally, the P-R man in business for himself has the greatest growth potential, but he also carries the greatest risk. Almost as lucrative is the status of account executive in a large public-relations office, but the life can be somewhat hectic because of the conflicting pressures that come simultaneously from the client and the media.

Very closely akin to the public-relations field is that of advertising. We would be the last ones to suggest that an advertising agency should specialize in real-estate accounts exclusively. The risk would be too great in the event the realty industry were to hit a slump. But many agencies have done rather well by establishing for themselves reputations for giving specialized and talented service to realty clients. This means that one or several of the executives in the agency are experts in this field.

Photography and Art

Not far removed from the writing field is that of the visual arts. To the extent that real estate calls for graphic presentation for sales and promotional purposes, the photographer and artist are much in demand.

Builders constantly call upon photographers to produce attractive pictures of their houses or buildings for sales literature and publicity. Many cameramen who specialize in this field have a loyal clientele among realty men. Some photographers have become justly famous for their excellent shots of exteriors and interiors of houses and larger structures. Their work is used not only in sales brochures and newspaper publicity but is often in great demand among magazines.

The artist, too, has his place in this business. A specialty that can be quite lucrative is that of the renderer. This calls for an understanding of architectual plans and specifications. For a renderer has to be able to take a set of plans and specifications, and from what they tell him produce a faithful drawing or painting of a structure as it will look upon completion. Good renderings are needed for a variety of uses. One is when a builder hopes to impress a mortgage lender with his project sufficiently to obtain a loan. Another is publicity in the various media. Since large buildings can be photographed only on completion—long after their sponsors begin to seek recognition for them—these structures must be portrayed by some means other than photography. This is where rendering comes in. Renderings are also used for poster displays and other graphic demonstrations. Most photographers and renderers are in business for themselves. The fees they charge depend entirely on the local market and upon their professional standing.

Law and Accounting

Turning away from the artistic fields, we come to some of the fringe professions. There is not sufficient opportunity here to discuss law and accounting fully. Let us therefore confine ourselves only to the role they play in the real-estate industry. Nearly every realty transaction—whether it is the sale of a home or a skyscraper —is made with the aid of lawyers. For simpler deals, a general law practice is enough. But when it comes to the complexities that are a part of such matters as leases, sales, and mortgages, a more intimate knowledge of real-estate law is required. Today, many law firms have at least one real-estate specialist. Also, some law firms and individual practitioners make real estate their specialty. In New York, as well as some other states, a lawyer is also entitled to act as a realty broker. This means that he can claim a broker's commission when he is instrumental in the sale or lease of a property. As a result, many lawyers become syndicators.

Accounting and tax law can also be developed as a real-estate specialty. And since there are a number of large firms of certified public accountants who concentrate on the realty industry, here is another field where specialists are in great demand. All over the country there is a shortage of good real-estate accountants, men who know the economic and tax implications of realty deals. This may seem surprising in view of the long history of real estate itself. But while accounting and tax law were once treated as a sort of auxiliary service, in more recent years they have become the heart and soul of real-estate matters. In large measure, this is due to the increasing role played by taxes in shaping real-estate transactions. To discuss fully all the preparations for a professional career in law or accounting is virtually impossible. Let us assume here that a lawyer or accountant works for a large law or accountancy firm. After handling the firm's general business for a number of years, the young lawyer or accountant who is so disposed should let his superiors know that he is particularly interested in the realty phase of his profession. In all likelihood, the real-estate matters that come into the office will soon be handed to him. Thus, he is on his way to becoming a realty specialist—a role he can pursue within the framework of the law or accounting firm or by establishing a practice of his own.

Architecture and Engineering

Two other professions are usually considered to be a part of the real-estate field—architecture and engineering. Here, too, these careers bear fuller discussion than we can offer. Architecture, of course, is extremely dependent on real estate itself because almost any structure an architect designs is, in effect, real estate. For the most part, the work of structural engineers parallels that of architects. For the construction of many large buildings structural engineers are called in to work with the architects on the design. Many of the big architectural firms have their own engineering departments, too. In addition to design work, there is another function in real estate that the engineer can perform profitably— inspection. This pursuit may take several forms. The most common career of an inspecting engineer lies in the service of a municipality. Before building plans can be approved to give a builder the green light to break ground, architects or engineers of the municipal building department must examine the blueprints and specifications to make certain the proposed structure is safe and conforms to the local code. Once construction has started, engineers assigned to field work make periodic checks at the site to see that the actual construction follows the standards approved on paper.

Engineers with similar duties are also employed by the federal government, specifically by the Federal Housing Administration; and as long as the G. I. Bill of Rights continues to guarantee veterans' home mortgages, there will also be jobs with the Veterans Administration. Federal inspectors are concerned with the basic quality of houses and other structures when mortgages on them are insured or guaranteed by the federal government. If a home builder, for instance, plans to obtain F.H.A. or V.A. financing for his houses, he must first submit to these agencies the plans of his model homes and the proposed subdivision of his land. When the project has been approved and he proceeds with the actual construction, these agencies send inspectors —most of them engineers—to check on the work. As for municipal employment and positions with the F.H.A. and other government branches that hire structural engineers for inspection purposes, employment, advancement, and pay scales are controlled by civil-service tables. Salaries vary from area to area, but they are seldom outside the range of $6,000 to $9,600.

A relatively new function of the inspecting engineer is that of the private consultant. To our knowledge, it is only about four years since the first professional engineer opened a private practice to advise home buyers on their choices. Today, there are at least three such firms active in the New York metropolitan area alone, and their number is very likely to grow rapidly. These private practitioners inform prospective home purchasers through advertisements and circulars of the service they perform. Home buyers then retain them to make a thorough inspection of the condition of the house they are about to buy. A few days after the inspection, the engineers submit a detailed report on the property. Unlike appraisers, the engineers do not concern themselves with monetary value, nor do they advise the client to buy or not to buy. That decision is left to the home seeker. The fees for such services vary with each inspection firm, but they are usually in the vicinity of $50 per inspection, depending on the size of the house and its distance from the engineer's office.

This service has met with an enthusiastic reception among prospective home buyers, who are naturally glad to pay these moderate fees before investing a lot of money in a home. And the engineers who have been providing this service conscientiously are now making very attractive incomes. The pioneer in the field began his work as a sideline to supplement his earnings in a general engineering concern. Within weeks, he found it necessary to quit his job to devote full time to his new profession. Today, engineers are retained not only by buyers of resale houses but also to check new houses that are being erected for their clients. They are also being called on increasingly by business concerns to inspect buildings before they invest in them.

Home Improvement

Home improvement is also big business nowadays. Time was when carpenters, plumbers, and electricians hired themselves out in their spare time or during periods of unemployment to add rooms or finish basements and attics for home owners. This is no longer the case, for home improvement today is a $15,000,000,000 industry. Although many well-organized home-improvement concerns are outgrowths of construction businesses, lumber yards, and such, the newest members of the industry devote their attention exclusively to improvement. They do not build houses. They do not make occasional repairs. Instead, they have elaborate showrooms where home owners get advice, a chance to examine the materials that go into home expansions, and estimates of what the job will cost. Today's leader in the home-improvement business is not a technician in overalls but an executive whose primary concern is effective management.

Interesting and lucrative careers await the young home-improvement specialist. It is a field, incidentally, that does not require a broad education. Given a talent for organization and the ability to make accurate price computations from a thorough knowledge of building materials and labor methods and output, a man can enter this business and be successful with little more than a high-school education. If he has sales talent, more power to him. But even without salesmanship, he can operate a successful business by hiring a sales force much as he hires technicians. And while the educational background is secondary—which does not mean that advanced education is not helpful—training in such fields as carpentry, plumbing, electrical work, masonry, and the like is naturally an aid.

We suggest that anyone planning to enter this field start by taking a job in the office of a home-improvement firm. This will familiarize him with the selling, estimating, and scheduling techniques that usually spell the difference between success and failure in this business. Depending on the duties assigned to a young recruit in the home-improvement business, his salary will range anywhere from $75 to $200 a week. The upper figure can be earned if he also takes a hand in selling improvement projects to customers; in that case, his income includes commissions.

If the employee feels competent after a time to open his own improvement business, his earnings are limited only by his efficiency and that of his sales and work force. There are, however, pretty much the same risks as those in the building business in general. A downturn in the economy induces home owners to postpone enlargement of their houses. Inefficient job planning, hasty estimating, overexpansion, needless overhead, and other setbacks can drive a careless improvement contractor bankrupt. But the recent growth of the field as an established business form is helping to reduce this risk by standardizing many of its procedures. Those who hesitate to undertake the risk, however, can still earn attractive incomes as employees. As the larger im-

provement concerns branch out, many rewarding exec:
tive positions will open up. Naturally, earnings of suc.
executives will be commensurate with their authority
and responsibility.

Home Maintenance

In the same way, home maintenance is becoming big
business. During the past three years, so-called home-
owner's clubs—actually substantial business enterprises
—have cropped up throughout the country. They so-
licit membership among home owners for relatively
modest dues, and when a home owner is in need of
home-repair service, he calls the club. The repairman
who is dispatched is one of the contractors with whom
the club deals regularly. He performs the work and is
paid by the club. The home owner is then billed by the
club at the end of the month. It is, in effect, a variation
of the credit-card system.

Some clubs have gone far beyond the home-main-
tenance field. A number of them service appliances and
even provide baby sitters. Their income is derived from
membership dues as well as a small markup on the contractors' service. Lately, too, the clubs have been offering memberships to owners of large, commercial buildings and to apartment dwellers. The most attractive incomes, of course, are those of the organizers of such
clubs. There are few executive positions in this field;
most of the employees are merely clerks, since the actual
work is done by outside subcontractors.

Surveying

In view of land's being the basis of real property, it is
only natural that it should give rise to a number of important realty careers. One of the first is that of the surveyor. His is one of the most essential functions in the
realty field. He is the man who determines where a given

piece of property begins and ends. Some surveyors pursue this profession as a side line to a general real-estate business. Others make it a full-time occupation. Surveying is a science, which is taught in a number of technical schools.

Surveyors are called on to determine the boundaries of land parcels for a variety of purposes. These include land sales, mapping for assessments and other objectives, and for public improvements. A surveyor who devotes his full time to this specialty can develop a fairly profitable practice by making surveys for real-estate men, lending institutions, and the like. The government also employs surveyors in the departments where they are needed, paying them according to civil-service schedules. The general real-estate practitioner who surveys as a side line is not likely to be called upon for many major projects, though he can still pick up some handsome fees locally from time to time.

Title Abstracting

Another occupation that is closely linked to land is that of the title abstracter. Since having a clear title to real property is essential to buying and selling real estate, finding out whether a title is clear of defects has become an occupation in itself. This involves detailed research into all public records that affect the title to a piece of property. These records include those of the county clerk, where deeds and mortgages are recorded; the various courts, where liens and litigations are filed; the tax bureaus, where tax liens are placed against property; and so forth. The actual searching is performed by a relatively low-salaried clerical employee. As a rule, each searcher is assigned to one set of records, such as certain dockets in the county clerk's office. For each title being searched, it is this man's job to look into his assigned records to find out if there are any entries that affect the property concerned. Once the searchers have indicated on the title record all they have found in the records, a lawyer or a specially trained abstracter in the title concern interprets the findings to give an opinion of the title. If this is done by an abstracter who is not a lawyer, any serious questions about the title must be submitted to a lawyer on the staff of the title company for interpretation.

A title company earns its profits in two possible ways. One is to sell the abstract to the people who ordered the title search, probably either a purchaser or a mortgage lender. The other is to insure the title. This means that the title company, after satisfying itself that the title is clear of any defects, issues an insurance policy that guarantees the beneficiary—the owner of the property or the holder of the mortgage—that he will not have to bear any loss should a defect ultimately show up in the title.

In some areas of the country, title companies play a less prominent role than others, especially in localities where the Torrens System is used. This system, which has ardent advocates as well as vehement opponents, provides a perpetual record of each title and is said to make title searching unnecessary. In some areas, title work is performed by so-called escrow companies that handle all of the legal and financing details of realty sales. Because mortgage financing includes establishing a clear title, many title companies combine both functions by acting as mortgage brokers as well. In effect, they are able to offer mortgages to lending institutions with the assurance that the titles on them are clear. In a title company concerned purely with searches and insurance, the only really attractive incomes are earned by those who have investments in the operation, the lawyers who determine the risk, and the salesmen who convince realty men and mortgage lenders to retain the title company for the search and insurance. If, in addition, a title company acts as mortgage broker, then all of the careers common to the mortgage business are also open.

Undoubtedly, other fields can be related to the real-estate industry, if only remotely. And as conditions change and new ideas are developed in various areas of the industry, new occupations will arise, too. But, as we said at the outset, real estate is one of the few fields in which a man or woman can start a general practice and turn to a specialty as readily as one can start as a specialist and turn to a general practice or to some other specialty. Because of this vast flexibility and the many opportunities this great industry offers to all kinds of people, the best advice we can give to enterprising men and women who are looking for interesting, varied, and rewarding work is— Try it!

CHAPTER VIII

Self-Evaluation Test

It is difficult to conceive of a personality that would not fit properly into some niche in this vast and varied field. However, simply because of the scope of real estate, it is impossible to apply a single personality test for the whole profession. Therefore, anyone who is contemplating a career in real estate would be wise to select that phase of the business in which he gets the highest score for affirmative answers to the questions below.

RESIDENTIAL BROKERAGE

1. Do you have the patience and understanding required to bear with families while they go through the often sensitive process of finding a home?

Yes_____ No_____

2. Would you be quick to deduce from a person's description—even if it's rather hazy—precisely what he needs and wants and can afford in terms of both a house and its location?

Yes_____ No_____

3. Could you act as a trusted middleman in bringing two parties together on price, knowing the problems of the buyer yet aware that you will be paid by the seller?

Yes_____ No_____

4. Are you aggressive enough to obtain listings from strangers who, you have reason to believe, are planning to sell their homes?

Yes_____   No_____

5. Considering that your income results from commissions on sales, could you adjust to living on fluctuating earnings rather than regular weekly pay?

Yes_____   No_____

COMMERCIAL BROKERAGE

1. Are you sufficiently aggressive to approach large business concerns that you think could be convinced to move if you were persuasive enough?

Yes_____   No_____

2. Do you have a detective's instinct, enabling you to read between the lines of news items and other information and discover when a firm is about to vacate its space or is seeking new space, so that you can act on your educated hunch before a competitor does?

Yes_____   No_____

3. Do you have the perseverance to work on a deal for months, perhaps even years, with the ever-present possibility that it may fall apart at any time, and still not lose your enthusiasm for the next transaction?

Yes_____   No_____

4. In working on putting together a large plot of land from various small owners, would you be capable of the cloak-and-dagger type of discretion needed to keep secret the name of the client and the purpose for which the land is being assembled?

Yes_____   No_____

5. Knowing that your income will come from commissions paid only for actual sales or leases, are you prepared to face the lean weeks and years as well as the fat ones?

Yes——— No———

MANAGEMENT

1. Do you have a mind for detail and the patience to follow through on the various problems that arise from running a property?

Yes——— No———

2. Are you prepared to make the rounds of buildings that you manage on those inclement days when everyone else is comfortable indoors?

Yes——— No———

3. Are you more inclined to earn your income by salary than by commission?

Yes——— No———

4. Could you handle the daily complaints, some justified and some not, of disgruntled tenants?

Yes——— No———

5. If you think you could, do you feel capable of handling them fairly, knowing that your first duty is to the owner of the building but being aware that the tenants have rights, too?

Yes——— No———

BUILDING

1. Do you like being outdoors?

Yes——— No———

2. Do you like rough work—wearing work clothes, and putting up with noise, commotion, and the like?

Yes——— No———

3. Can you live at ease without any certainty that what you are building will provide you with a satisfactory income—in short, that it could flop?

Yes_____ No_____

4. Are you sufficiently flexible to adjust what you would like to build to what your prospective customers or tenants want you to build?

Yes_____ No_____

5. Do you feel that you could convince an investor, a mortgage lender, or some other backer that your project is worth backing if you believe it is?

Yes_____ No_____

FINANCING AND ALLIED FIELDS

1. Do you have a flair for financial transactions?

Yes_____ No_____

2. Do you have the imagination to take the elements of what appears to be a routine real-estate situation and endow it with enough interest and appeal to make it a tempting financial package?

Yes_____ No_____

3. Could you correlate rigid tables of value with your own sense of property values to make reasonable and accurate appraisals?

Yes_____ No_____

4. Is your interest in realty such that you would like to apply your knowledge to a city, state, or federal-government career with its high degree of security?

Yes_____ No_____

5. Is your interest in realty of a type that would enable you to use other talents, such as photography or writing, to find a career in a related field?

Yes_____ No_____

More ARCO Books
for School and Career Guidance

THE STUDENT'S GUIDE
Sir John Adams
Knowing the right way to study is half the battle; and this book, written for high school and college students contains many suggestions, procedures and guidelines to help you master **any** subject. Included are study schedules, memory techniques, reading abilities, use of text and reference books, note taking, essay writing, preparing for examinations and more. "For the student with intellect and curiosity, this book has sparkling but sound suggestions on how to be not only a good student but a good person."—**Choice. ($1.45)**

HOW TO BECOME A SUCCESSFUL STUDENT
Otis D. Froe & Maurice A. Lee
A practical guide in methods of study and learning. This book will help you to learn how to read and listen effectively, take quizzes and tests, use educational resources and facilities, reach the top in scholastic efficiency, learn the most with a minimum of effort and time, take good notes and set up a study schedule. **($1.25)**

COLLEGIAN'S GUIDE TO PART-TIME EMPLOYMENT
Russell Granger
A factual guide for all those students who want to work part-time while going to college. Information about the jobs available, how much time they take, what they pay and how to apply for them. Suggestions for operating a small business of your own are also included. **(95c)**

FIND YOUR JOB AND LAND IT
Leonard Corwen
You'll learn how to evaluate your education and experience, prepare resumes to reflect your strongest assets, write and answer ads, use the facilities of employment agencies, and make a good impression at interviews. Whether you are looking for your first job or for a better one, this book offers professional pointers on how to sell yourself to prospective employers. **(95c)**